Celebration

**Combined
Sound of Living Waters
Fresh Sounds
Cry Hosanna**

Words only edition

Compiled by

**Mimi Farra
Betty Pulkingham
Jeanne Harper**

HODDER AND STOUGHTON
LONDON   SYDNEY   AUCKLAND   TORONTO

British Library Cataloguing in Publication Data

Celebration: combined Sound of Living Waters,
    Fresh Sounds and Cry Hosanna. – Words
    only ed.
1. Hymns, English
  I. Harper, Jeanne   II. Pulkingham, Betty
 III. Farra, Mimi   IV. Sound of living waters
  V. Fresh sounds   VI. Cry Hosanna
 264'.2   BV459

ISBN 0 340 39391 2

Copyright © 1986 by Jeanne Harper, Betty Pulkingham and Mimi Farra. First printed 1986. Third impression 1988. All rights reserved. No part of this publication may be reproduced or transmitted in any form or by any means, electronically or mechanically, including photocopying, recording or any information storage or retrieval system, without prior permission in writing from the publisher. This publication is not included under licences issued by the Copyright Licensing Agency. Printed in Great Britain for Hodder and Stoughton Limited, Mill Road, Dunton Green, Sevenoaks, Kent by Richard Clay Ltd, Bungay, Suffolk. Photoset by Rowland Phototypesetting Ltd, Bury St Edmunds, Suffolk. Hodder and Stoughton Editorial Office: 47 Bedford Square London WC1B 3DP.

CONTENTS

Sound of Living Waters

1	Hallelujah! . . . songs of praise and thanksgiving	1–18
2	Kneel and adore . . . songs of worship	19–32
3	Look up . . . songs of hope and vision	33–44
4	Become . . . wholeness and maturity	45–52
5	Songs of the kingdom . . . the body of Christ	53–69
6	Suffer-Reign . . . songs of faith and victory	70–81
7	Go forth . . . outreach	82–92
8	Sing a Psalm	93–101
9	Come as children . . . songs for children of all ages	102–111
10	Songs for a season	112–127

Fresh Sounds

1	Hallelujah! . . . songs of praise and thanksgiving	128–141
2	Kneel and adore . . . songs of worship	142–158
3	Liturgical songs	159–172
4	Become . . . songs of wholeness and maturity	173–183
5	Songs of the kingdom . . . the body of Christ	184–196
6	Suffer-Reign . . . songs of faith and victory	197–206
7	Come as children . . . songs for children of all ages	207–222
8	Go forth . . . songs of outreach	223–234

Cry Hosanna

1	Songs of praise and thanksgiving	235–258
2	Songs of worship	259–273
3	Songs of hope, vision and wholeness	274–288
4	Songs of the kingdom	289–306
5	Songs of faith and victory	307–319
6	Songs of outreach	320–328
7	Songs for children	329–343
8	Psalms	344–358
9	Seasonal songs	359–376

COPYRIGHT ACKNOWLEDGEMENTS
INDEX OF TITLES AND FIRST LINES

The songs in this combined words edition have been renumbered from 1 to 376. The original number of each song in its source book appears below the author's name at the head of each item.

SOUND OF LIVING WATERS

1   Don Fishel / SLW 1

Refrain
Alleluia, alleluia, give thanks to the risen Lord,
Alleluia, alleluia, give praise to his name.

Jesus is Lord of all the earth.
    He is the King of creation.

Spread the good news o'er all the earth.
    Jesus has died and has risen.

We have been crucified with Christ.
    Now we shall live for ever.

God has proclaimed the just reward,
    Life for all men, alleluia.

Come let us praise the living God,
    Joyfully sing to our Saviour.

2   Pat Uhl Howard / SLW 2

Refrain
O what a gift! What a wonderful gift!
Who can tell the wonders of the Lord?
Let us open our eyes, our ears, and our hearts;
    It is Christ the Lord, it is he!

In the stillness of the night
When the world was asleep,
The almighty Word leapt out.
He came to Mary, he came to us,
Christ came to the land of Galilee.
    Christ our Lord and our King!

On the night before he died
It was Passover night,
And he gathered his friends together.
He broke the bread, he blessed the wine;
It was the gift of his love and his life.
    Christ our Lord and our King!

On the hill of Calvary
The world held its breath,
For there for the world to see,
God gave his Son, his very own Son
For the love of you and me.
    Christ our Lord and our King!

Early on that morning
When the guards were sleeping,
Back to life came he!
He conquered death, he conquered sin,
But the vict'ry he gave to you and me!
    Christ our Lord and our King!

Some day with the saints
We will come before our Father
And then we will shout and dance and sing.
For in our midst for our eyes to see
Will be Christ our Lord and our King!
    Christ our Lord and our King!

3   Anon. / SLW 3

Something in my heart
    like a stream running free
Makes me feel so happy,
    as happy as can be;
When I think of Jesus
    and what he's done for me,
Something in my heart
    like a stream running free.

4   Anon. / SLW 4

Give me oil in my lamp, keep me burning.
Give me oil in my lamp, I pray.
Give me oil in my lamp, keep me burning,
Keep me burning 'til the break of day.

Refrain
Sing hosanna, sing hosanna,
Sing hosanna to the King of kings!

Make me a fisher of men, keep me seeking . . .

Give me joy in my heart, keep me singing . . .

Give me love in my heart, keep me serving . . .

5   John Newton / SLW 5

Amazing grace! How sweet the sound
    That saved a wretch like me.
I once was lost, but now am found,
    Was blind, but now I see.

'Twas grace that taught my heart to fear,
  And grace my fears relieved.
How precious did that grace appear
  The hour I first believed.

Through many dangers, toils and snares,
  I have already come;
'Tis grace hath brought me safe thus far,
  And grace will lead me home.

When we've been there ten thousand years,
  Bright shining as the sun,
We've no less days to sing God's praise,
  Than when we've first begun.

6   Anon.
SLW 6

Refrain
Oh! Oh! Oh! how good is the Lord.
(3 times)
I never will forget what he has done for me.

He gives me salvation, how good is the Lord.
(3 times)
I never will forget what he has done for me.

He gives me his blessings . . .

He gives me his Spirit . . .

He gives me his healing . . .

He gives me his glory . . .

7   Max Dyer
SLW 7

I will sing, I will sing a song unto the Lord.
(3 times)
Alleluia, glory to the Lord.

Refrain
Allelu, alleluia, glory to the Lord. *(3 times)*
Alleluia, glory to the Lord.

Optional verses:
We will come, we will come
  as one before the Lord.
  Alleluia, glory to the Lord.

If the Son, if the Son shall make you free,
  You shall be free indeed.

They that sow in tears shall reap in joy.
  Alleluia, glory to the Lord.

Every knee shall bow
  and every tongue confess
That Jesus Christ is Lord.

In his name, in his name we have the victory.
  Alleluia, glory to the Lord.

8   Brian Howard
SLW 8

Refrain
Let us give thanks
That our names are written,
Let us give thanks
That our names are written,
Written in the book of life,
Inscribed upon his palms,
Written in the book of life,
Inscribed upon his palms.

Rejoice not that devils flee in his name.
Rejoice not in the power that he gave;
For he came to break the bonds of sin.
Yes he did, he came to set us free,
  so freely we sing.

For he came to give us life,
That we might have it more abundantly;
Came to break the power of sin, he did.
Yes, he did, he came to set us free,
  so freely we sing.

Let us give thanks,
Thanks unto the Father,
Thanks unto the Son,
Thanks to the Holy Spirit,
Our Lord God Three in One.

9   Eleanor Farjeon
SLW 9

Morning has broken like the first morning;
  Blackbird has spoken like the first bird.
Praise for the singing! Praise for the morning!
  Praise for them springing
    fresh from the word.

Sweet the rain's new fall, sunlit from heaven,
  Like the first dew fall on the first grass.
Praise for the sweetness of the wet garden,
  Sprung in completeness
    where his feet pass.

Mine is the sunlight! Mine is the morning;
  Born of the one light Eden saw play.
Praise with elation! Praise every morning
  God's re-creation of the new day.

10 Evelyn Tarner
SLW **10**

Rejoice in the Lord always,
  and again I say rejoice.
Rejoice in the Lord always,
  and again I say rejoice.
Rejoice, rejoice, and again I say rejoice.
Rejoice, rejoice, and again I say rejoice.

11 Joachim Neander
SLW **11**

Praise to the Lord, the almighty,
  the King of creation;
O my soul, praise him for he is thy health
    and salvation;
  Join the great throng,
  Psaltery, organ and song,
Sounding in glad adoration.

Praise to the Lord, over all things
  he gloriously reigneth;
Borne as on eagle wings,
  safely his saints he sustaineth.
  Hast thou not seen
  How all thou needest hath been
Granted in what he ordaineth?

Praise to the Lord, who doth prosper thy way
  and defend thee;
Surely his goodness and mercy
  shall ever attend thee;
  Ponder anew
  What the almighty can do,
Who with his love doth befriend thee.

Praise to the Lord! O let all that is in me
  adore him!
All that hath breath join with Abraham's seed
  to adore him!
  Let the 'Amen'
  Sum all our praises again
Now as we worship before him.

12 Francis Pott
SLW **12**

Angel voices ever singing
  Round thy throne of light,
Angel harps for ever ringing,
  Rest not day nor night;
Thousands only live to bless thee,
And confess thee
  Lord of might.

Thou who art beyond the farthest
  Mortal eye can scan.
Can it be that thou regardest
  Songs of sinful man?
Can we know that thou art near us
And wilt hear us?
  Yes, we can.

Yes, we know that thou rejoicest
  O'er each work of thine;
Thou didst ears and hands and voices
  For thy praise design;
Craftsman's art and music's measure
For thy pleasure
  All combine.

In thy house, great God, we offer
  Of thine own to thee;
And for thine acceptance proffer
  All unworthily,
Hearts and minds and hands and voices
In our choicest
  Psalmody.

Honour, glory, might, and merit
  Thine shall ever be,
Father, Son, and Holy Spirit,
  Blessed Trinity.
Of the best that thou hast given
Earth and heaven
  Render thee.

13 Les Garrett
SLW **13**

This is the day, this is the day
  that the Lord has made,
  that the Lord has made.
We will rejoice, we will rejoice
  and be glad in it, and be glad in it.
This is the day that the Lord has made.
We will rejoice and be glad in it.
This is the day that the Lord has made.

This is the day when he rose again . . .

This is the day when the Spirit came . . .

CELEBRATION

14 Anon.
SLW 14

Praise him, praise him,
Praise him in the morning,
Praise him in the noontime,
Praise him, praise him,
Praise him when the sun goes down.

Jesus . . .

Love him . . .

Trust him . . .

Serve him . . .

15 Mimi Farra
SLW 15

Refrain
Hallelujah! Hallelujah! Hallelujah!
    Jesus is Lord!
Hallelujah! Hallelujah! Hallelujah!
    Jesus is King!

All gather round the throne of the Lamb,
    His praises sing throughout eternity.

Lift up your voice with the thousands who cry:
    'Worthy, worthy art thou, Lamb of God.'

Blessing and honour and glory and pow'r
    Be unto him for ever and ever.

All glory be to the one Triune God,
    The Father, Son, and the – Holy Spirit.

16 Anon.
SLW 16

Jesus Christ is alive today
[I/We] know, [I/We] know it's true.
Sovereign of the universe,
[I/We] give him homage due.
Seated there at God's right hand,
[I am/We are] with him in the promised land.
Jesus lives and reigns in [me/you.]
That's how I know it's true.

17 Charles Wesley
SLW 17

O for a thousand tongues to sing
    My great redeemer's praise,
The glories of my God and King,
    The triumphs of his grace.

Jesus! the name that charms our fears,
    That bids our sorrows cease;
'Tis music in the sinner's ears,
    'Tis life, and health, and peace.

He breaks the power of cancelled sin,
    He sets the prisoner free;
His blood can make the foulest clean,
    His blood availed for me.

He speaks, and listening to his voice,
    New life the dead receive,
The mournful, broken hearts rejoice,
    The humble poor believe.

Hear him, ye deaf; his praise, ye dumb,
    Your loosened tongues employ;
Ye blind, behold your Saviour come;
    And leap, ye lame, for joy!

My gracious master and my God,
    Assist me to proclaim,
To spread through all the earth abroad
    The honours of thy name.

18 Anon.
SLW 18

Thank you, thank you, Jesus.
Thank you, thank you, Jesus.
Thank you, thank you, Jesus, in my heart.
Thank you, thank you, Jesus.
Oh, thank you, thank you, Jesus.
Thank you, thank you, Jesus, in my heart.

You can't make me doubt him.
You can't make me doubt him in my heart.
You can't make me doubt him,
I know too much about him.
Thank you, thank you, Jesus, in my heart.

I can't live without him.
I can't live without him in my heart.
I can't live without him,
I know too much about him.
Thank you, thank you, Jesus, in my heart.

Glory, hallelujah!
Glory, hallelujah, in my heart!
Glory, hallelujah!
Glory, hallelujah!
Thank you, thank you, Jesus, in my heart!

19 Jimmy Owens
SLW 19

Holy, holy, holy, holy.
Holy, holy, Lord God Almighty;

And we lift our hearts before you
    as a token of our love,
        Holy, holy, holy, holy.

Gracious Father, gracious Father,
We're so glad to be your children,
    gracious Father;
And we lift our heads before you
    as a token of our love,
        Gracious Father, gracious Father.

Precious Jesus, precious Jesus,
We're so glad that you've redeemed us,
    precious Jesus,
And we lift our hands before you
    as a token of our love,
        Precious Jesus, precious Jesus.

Holy Spirit, Holy Spirit,
Come and fill our hearts anew, Holy Spirit,
And we lift our voice before you
    as a token of our love,
        Holy Spirit, Holy Spirit.

Repeat first verse.

Hallelujah, hallelujah, hallelujah, hallelujah,
And we lift our hearts before you
    as a token of our love.
        Hallelujah, hallelujah.

20   Anon. / SLW 20

Let all that is within me cry, 'Holy.'
Let all that is within me cry, 'Holy.'
Holy, holy, holy is the Lamb that was slain.

Let all that is within me cry, 'Worthy' . . .

Let all that is within me cry, 'Jesus' . . .

Let all that is within me cry, 'Glory' . . .

21   Oressa Wise / SLW 21

Son of God, Son of God,
We come before you
To love and adore you,
Son of God.

Word of God, Word of God,
We come to hear you,
To always be near you,
Word of God.

Lamb of God, Lamb of God,
We come to bless you,
To ever confess you,
Lamb of God.

Repeat first verse.

22   Gerhardt Tersteegen / SLW 22

God himself is with us,
    Let us all adore him,
And with awe appear before him.
God is here within us:
    Soul in silence fear him,
Humbly, fervently draw near him.
    Now his own who have known
God, in worship lowly,
    Yield their spirits wholly.

Come, abide within me;
    Let my soul, like Mary,
Be thine earthly sanctuary.
Come, indwelling Spirit,
    With transfigured splendour;
Love and honour will I render,
    Where I go here below,
Let me bow before thee,
    Know thee, and adore thee.

Gladly we surrender
    Earth's deceitful treasures,
Pride of life, and sinful pleasures:
Gladly, Lord, we offer
    Thine to be for ever,
Soul and life and each endeavour,
    Thou alone shalt be known
Lord of all our being,
    Life's true way decreeing.

23   Anon. / SLW 23

We see the Lord,
We see the Lord,
And he is high and lifted up,
And his train fills the temple.
He is high and lifted up,
And his train fills the temple.
The angels cry, 'Holy',
The angels cry, 'Holy',
The angels cry, 'Holy is the Lord.'

CELEBRATION

24   Anon.   SLW 24

He is Lord, he is Lord,
He is risen from the dead, and he is Lord.
Every knee shall bow,
Every tongue confess
That Jesus Christ is Lord.

25   Anon.   SLW 25

Alleluia. *(8 times)*

How I love him.

Blessed Jesus.

My Redeemer

Jesus is Lord.

Alleluia.

26   Terrye Coelho   SLW 26

Father, we adore you;
Lay our lives before you.
How we love you.

Jesus we adore you . . .

Spirit we adore you . . .

27   Anon.   SLW 27

Thank you, thank you, Jesus.
Thank you, thank you, Jesus.
Oh, thank you, thank you, Jesus in my heart.
Thank you, thank you, Jesus.
Oh, thank you, thank you, Jesus.
Oh, thank you, thank you, Jesus, in my heart.

Love you, love you, Jesus.
Love you, love you, Jesus.
Oh, love you, love you, Jesus in my heart . . .

Father, God almighty.
Father, God almighty,
Oh, Father, God almighty, take my heart . . .

Glory hallelujah!
Glory hallelujah!
Oh, glory hallelujah in my heart . . .

28   Pauline Michael Mills and Tom Smail   SLW 28

Thou art worthy, thou art worthy,
   Thou art worthy, O Lord.
Thou art worthy to receive glory,
   Glory and honour and power.
For thou hast created, hast all things created,
   For thou hast created all things.
And for thy pleasure they are created;
   Thou art worthy, O Lord.

Thou art worthy, thou art worthy,
   Thou art worthy, O Lamb.
Thou art worthy to receive glory,
   And power at the Father's right hand.
For thou hast redeemed us,
   hast ransomed and cleaned us
By thy blood setting us free;
In white robes arrayed us,
   kings and priests made us,
And we are reigning in thee.

29   Daniel Iverson   SLW 29

Spirit of the living God, fall afresh on me.
Spirit of the living God, fall afresh on me.
Break me, melt me, mould me, fill me.
Spirit of the living God, fall afresh on me.

30   Anon.   SLW 30

Jesus, Jesus, Jesus,
Never have I heard a name
   that thrills my soul like thine.
Jesus, Jesus, Jesus,
Oh, what matchless grace that links that
   precious name with mine.

31   Sylvia Lawton   SLW 32

Jesus, Jesus, wonderful Lord,
Gently you touched me
   and made my life whole;
How can I thank you except that I see
Your way of life is truly for me?

Jesus, Jesus, take my life,
Jesus, Jesus, I give to you
All things, always yours to become.
Jesus my Saviour, I will be thine.

Seeing, looking with new eyes;
Loving, caring just as you do;
Learning all things from your point of view;
Lord Jesus Christ, your touch is so true.

32 Andrew Reed
SLW **33**

Spirit divine, attend our prayers,
  And make this house thy home;
Descend with all thy gracious powers,
  O come, great Spirit, come!

Come as the light; to us reveal
  Our emptiness and woe,
And lead us in those paths of life
  Whereon the righteous go.

Come as the fire, and purge our hearts
  Like sacrificial flame;
Let our whole soul an offering be
  To our redeemer's name.

Come as the dove, and spread thy wings,
  The wings of peaceful love;
And let thy Church on earth become
  Blest as the Church above.

Spirit divine, attend our prayers;
  Make a lost world thy home;
Descend with all thy gracious powers;
  O come, great Spirit, come!

33 Kathleen Thomerson
SLW **34**

I want to walk as a child of the light.
I want to follow Jesus.
God set the stars to give light to the world.
The star of my life is Jesus.

Refrain
In him there is no darkness at all,
  The night and the day are both alike.
The Lamb is the light of the city of God.
  Shine in my heart, Lord Jesus.

I want to see the brightness of God.
I want to look at Jesus.
Clear sun of righteousness, shine on my path,
And show me the way to the Father.

I'm looking for the coming of Christ.
I want to be with Jesus.
When we have run with patience the race,
We shall know the joy of Jesus.

34 John Oxenham
SLW **35**

In Christ there is no east or west,
  In him no south or north,
But one great fellowship of love
  Throughout the whole wide earth.

In him shall true hearts everywhere
  Their high communion find;
His service is the golden cord
  Close binding all mankind.

Join hands then, brothers of the faith,
  Whate'er your race may be;
Who serves my Father as a son
  Is surely kin to me.

In Christ now meet both east and west,
  In him meet south and north.
All Christly souls are one in him
  Throughout the whole wide earth.

35 American folk hymn
SLW **36**

Lord, I want to be a Christian,
  In-a my heart, in-a my heart.
Lord, I want to be a Christian,
  In-a my heart.
In-a my heart, in-a my heart,
Lord, I want to be a Christian in-a my heart.

Lord, I want to be more loving . . .

Lord, I want to be like Jesus . . .

Lord, I want to praise you freely . . .

36 Richard of Chichester and Jeanne Harper
SLW **37**

Day by day, dear Lord, of thee
  three things I pray:
To see thee more clearly,
To love thee more dearly,
To follow thee more nearly day by day.

Day by day, dear Lord, of thee
  three things I pray:
To trust thee more fully,
To leave things more wholly,
To lean on thee securely day by day.

CELEBRATION

37 — Richard of Chichester — SLW 38

Day by day,
O dear Lord, three things I pray:
  To see thee more clearly,
  Love thee more dearly,
  Follow thee more nearly,
Day by day.

38 — Bill Harmon — SLW 39

Reach out and touch the Lord as he goes by.
You'll find he's not too busy
  to hear your heart's cry.
He's passing by this moment
  your needs to supply.
Reach out and touch the Lord as he goes by.

39 — Anon. — SLW 40

I want to live for Jesus every day.
I want to live for Jesus, come what may.
Take the world and all its pleasure,
I've got a more enduring treasure.
I want to live for Jesus every day.

I'm gonna' live for Jesus every day . . .

40 — Author unknown — SLW 41

He shall teach you all things,
He shall teach you all things,
And bring all things to your remembrance,
  And bring all things to your remembrance.

41 — Traditional spiritual — SLW 42

✓

Kum ba yah, my Lord, Kum ba yah,
Kum ba yah, my Lord, Kum ba yah;
Kum ba yah, my Lord, Kum ba yah,
  O Lord, Kum ba yah.

Someone's crying, Lord, Kum ba yah . . .

Someone's singing, Lord, Kum ba yah . . .

Someone's praying, Lord, Kum ba yah . . .

42 — Bessie Porter Head — SLW 43

O Breath of Life, come sweeping through us,
  Revive thy Church with life and power.
O Breath of Life, come, cleanse, renew us,
  And fit thy Church to meet this hour.

O Wind of God, come bend us, break us,
  Till humbly we confess our need:
Then in thy tenderness re-make us,
  Revive, restore; for this we plead.

O Breath of Love, come breathe within us,
  Renewing thought and will and heart;
Come, love of Christ, afresh to win us,
  Revive thy Church in every part.

Revive us, Lord! Is zeal abating
  While harvest fields are vast and white?
Revive us, Lord, the world is waiting,
  Equip thy Church to spread the light.

43 — Jan Struther — SLW 44

Lord of all hopefulness, Lord of all joy,
Whose trust, ever childlike,
  no cares could destroy,
Be there at our waking, and give us, we pray,
Your bliss in our hearts, Lord,
  at the break of the day.

Lord of all eagerness, Lord of all faith,
Whose strong hands were skilled at the plane
  and the lathe,
Be there at our labours, and give us, we pray,
Your strength in our hearts, Lord,
  at the noon of the day.

Lord of all kindliness, Lord of all grace,
Your hands swift to welcome,
  your arms to embrace,
Be there at our homing, and give us, we pray,
Your love in our hearts, Lord,
  at the eve of the day.

Lord of all gentleness, Lord of all calm,
Whose voice is contentment,
  whose presence is balm,
Be there at our sleeping, and give us, we pray,
Your peace in our hearts, Lord,
  at the end of the day.

44
Caroline M. Noel
SLW 45 & 46

At the name of Jesus
  Every knee shall bow,
Every tongue confess him
  King of glory now.
'Tis the Father's pleasure
  We should call him Lord,
Who from the beginning
  Was the mighty Word.

Humbled for a season,
  To receive a name
From the lips of sinners,
  Unto whom he came,
Faithfully he bore it,
  Spotless to the last,
Brought it back victorious,
  When from death he passed.

Bore it up triumphant,
  With its human light,
Through all ranks of creatures,
  To the central height,
To the throne of Godhead,
  To the Father's breast;
Filled it with the glory
  Of that perfect rest.

In your hearts enthrone him,
  There let him subdue
All that is not holy,
  All that is not true:
Crown him as your captain
  In temptation's hour;
Let his will enfold you
  In its light and power.

Brothers, this Lord Jesus
  Shall return again,
With his Father's glory
  O'er the earth to reign;
For all wreaths of empire
  Meet upon his brow,
And our hearts confess him
  King of glory now.

45
St. Paul's Erith 1964 House Party
SLW 47

I want to walk with Jesus Christ,
  All the days I live of this life on earth,
To give to him complete control
  Of body and of soul.

Refrain
Follow him, follow him, yield your life to him,
  He has conquered death, he is King of kings.
Accept the joy which he gives to those
  Who yield their lives to him.

I want to learn to speak to him,
  To pray to him, confess my sin,
To open my life and let him in,
  For joy will then be mine.

I want to learn to speak of him,
  My life must show that he lives in me.
My deeds, my thoughts, my words must speak
  All of his love for me.

I want to learn to read his word,
  For this is how I know the way
To live my life as pleases him,
  In holiness and joy.

O Holy Spirit of the Lord,
  Enter now into this heart of mine,
Take full control of my selfish will
  And make me wholly thine.

46
John Newton
SLW 48

How sweet the name of Jesus sounds
  In a believer's ear!
It soothes his sorrows, heals his wounds,
  And drives away his fear.

It makes the wounded spirit whole,
  And calms the troubled breast;
'Tis manna to the hungry soul,
  And to the weary rest.

Dear name, the rock on which I build,
  My shield and hiding place,
My never-failing treasury, filled
  With boundless stores of grace.

Jesus! My Shepherd, Brother, Friend,
  My Prophet, Priest, and King,
My Lord, my life, my way, my end,
  Accept the praise I bring.

Weak is the effort of my heart,
  And cold my warmest thought;
But when I see thee as thou art,
  I'll praise thee as I ought.

Till then I would thy love proclaim
  With every fleeting breath;
And may the music of thy name
  Refresh my soul in death.

CELEBRATION

47 Anon.
SLW 49

Here comes Jesus, see him walking
    on the water,
    He'll lift you up and he'll help you to stand.
Here comes Jesus, he's the master
    of the waves that roll.
    Here comes Jesus, he'll make you whole.

Repeat in ascending keys, ending with the following (extra) words:

Here comes Jesus, he'll save your soul.

48 Anon.
SLW 50

Verse
Peter and John went to pray,
    they met a lame man on the way.
He asked for alms and held out his palms,
    and this is what Peter did say:

Refrain
'Silver and gold have I none,
    but such as I have give I thee.
In the name of Jesus Christ
    of Nazareth, rise up and walk!'

He went walking and leaping
    and praising God,
    walking and leaping and praising God.
'In the name of Jesus Christ
    of Nazareth, rise up and walk.'

49 North American spiritual
SLW 51

Refrain
There is a balm in Gilead
    to make the wounded whole.
There is a balm in Gilead
    to heal the sin-sick soul.

Sometimes I feel discouraged,
    and think my work's in vain,
but then the Holy Spirit
    revives my soul again.

If you cannot sing like angels,
    if you cannot preach like Paul,
you can tell the love of Jesus
    and say he died for all.

50 John Greenleaf Whittier
SLW 52

Dear Lord and Father of mankind,
    Forgive our foolish ways!
Reclothe us in our rightful mind;
    In purer lives thy service find,
In deeper rev'rence praise.

In simple trust like theirs who heard,
    Beside the Syrian sea,
The gracious calling of the Lord,
    Let us like them, without a word,
Rise up and follow thee.

O sabbath rest by Galilee!
    O calm of hills above,
Where Jesus knelt to share with thee
    The silence of eternity,
Interpreted by love.

With that deep hush subduing all
    Our words and works that drown
The tender whisper of thy call,
    As noiseless let thy blessing fall
As fell thy manna down.

Drop thy still dews of quietness
    Till all our strivings cease:
Take from our souls the strain and stress,
    And let our ordered lives confess
The beauty of thy peace.

Breathe through the heats of our desire
    Thy coolness and thy balm;
Let sense be dumb, let flesh retire;
    Speak through the earthquake,
        wind and fire,
O still small voice of calm.

51 Symphony of souls
SLW 53

You gotta have love in your heart.
You gotta have love in your heart.
You knew it was Jesus right from the start.
You gotta have love in your heart.

You gotta have peace on your mind.
You knew it was Jesus there all the time.

You gotta have joy in your soul.
The love of Jesus will make you whole.

La la la la . . .

52   Pamela Greenwood
       SLW **54**

By your stripes, Lord, I'm healed, hallelujah!
In your word it is revealed, hallelujah!
Yes, you bore it all for me,
     on the cross of Calvary
So that now I can go free, hallelujah!

53   William Dix
       SLW **55**

Alleluia! Sing to Jesus!
   His the sceptre, his the throne;
Alleluia! His the triumph,
   His the victory alone;
Hark! The songs of peaceful Zion
   Thunder like a mighty flood;
Jesus out of every nation
   Hath redeemed us by his blood.

Alleluia! Not as orphans
   Are we left in sorrow now;
Alleluia! He is near us,
   Faith believes, nor questions how:
Though the cloud from sight received him,
   When the forty days were o'er,
Shall our hearts forget his promise,
   'I am with you evermore'?

Alleluia! Bread of heaven,
   Thou on earth our food, our stay!
Alleluia! Here the sinful
   Flee to thee from day to day:
Intercessor, friend of sinners,
   Earth's redeemer, plead for me,
Where the songs of all the sinless
   Sweep across the crystal sea.

Alleluia! King eternal,
   Thee the Lord of lords we own:
Alleluia! Born of Mary,
   Earth thy footstool, heav'n thy throne
Thou within the veil hast entered,
   Robed in flesh, our great high priest:
Thou on earth both priest and victim
   In the eucharistic feast.

Alleluia! Sing to Jesus!
   His the sceptre, his the throne;
Alleluia! His the triumph,
   His the victory alone;
Hark! The songs of holy Zion
   Thunder like a mighty flood;
Jesus out of every nation
   Hath redeemed us by his blood.

54   Alan Teage
       SLW **56**

Blow, thou cleansing wind from heaven,
   Burn, thou fire, within our hearts.
Spirit of the Lord, possess us,
   Fill our lives in every part.
Mind of Christ, be thou our ruler.
   Word of truth, be thou our guide;
Leave no part of us unhallowed.
   Come, O come in us abide.

Fill thy Church, inspire and strengthen,
   Chasten, mould, empower and lead.
Make us one, and make us joyful,
   Give us grace for every need.
Be our life, build firm thy kingdom.
   Be our strength, who are but frail.
Then indeed against us never
   Shall the gates of hell prevail.

Win the world! Baptise the nations!
   Open every blinded eye.
Leave no sinner unconvicted;
   Leave no soul untouched and dry.
Conquering love, take thou the kingdom,
   Rule thou over all our days;
Then in glory and rejoicing
   Earth shall echo with thy praise.

55   Debby Kerner
       SLW **57**

Jesus. *(5 times)*

He died.

He rose.

He lives.

We live through him.

Jesus.

56   Karen Lafferty
       SLW **58**

Seek ye first the kingdom of God,
   And his righteousness,
And all these things shall be added unto you;
   Allelu, alleluia.

Alleluia, alleluia, alleluia,
   Allelu, Alleluia.

CELEBRATION

57
Priscilla Wright
SLW 59

Refrain
Fear not, rejoice and be glad,
The Lord hath done a great thing;
Hath poured out his Spirit on all mankind,
On those who confess his name.

The fig tree is budding, the vine beareth fruit,
    The wheat fields are golden with grain,
Thrust in the sickle, the harvest is ripe,
    The Lord has given us rain.

Ye shall eat in plenty and be satisfied,
    The mountains will drip with sweet wine,
My children shall drink of the fountain of life,
    My children will know they are mine.

My people shall know that I am the Lord,
    Their shame I have taken away.
My Spirit will lead them together again,
    My Spirit will show them the way.

My children shall dwell in a body of love,
    A light to the world they will be:
Life shall come forth from the Father above,
    My body will set mankind free.

58
Anon.; (Verses 2,3,4: Hong Sit)
SLW 60

God is building a house,
    God is building a house,
    God is building a house that will stand.
He is building by his plan
    With the lively stones of man,
God is building a house that will stand.

God is building a house,
    God is building a house,
    God is building a house that will stand.
With apostles, prophets, pastors,
    With evangelists and teachers,
God is building a house that will stand.

Christ is head of this house,
    Christ is head of this house,
    Christ is head of this house that will stand.
He abideth in its praise,
    Will perfect it in its ways,
Christ is head of this house that will stand.

We are part of this house,
    we are part of this house,
We are part of this house that will stand.
We are called from every nation
    To enjoy his full salvation,
We are part of this house that will stand.

59
Brian Howard
SLW 61

The kingdom of God is neither lo here,
    nor lo there,
    No, the kingdom is among us.

The victory of God is neither lo here,
    nor lo there,
    No, the victory is among us.

The power of God is neither lo here,
    nor lo there,
    No, the power is among us.

The Spirit of God was not lost after Pentecost,
    No, the Spirit is among us.

The Prince of peace has not gone away,
    he won't let you stray,
    No, the Prince of peace is among us.

The joy of the Lord is like a singing lark,
    deep within your heart,
    Let it flow so freely among us.

60
Author unknown
SLW 63

I am the bread of life;
He who/ comes to me shall not hunger;
He who be/lieves in me shall not thirst.
No-one can come to me
Un/ less the Father draw him.

Refrain
And I will raise him up (*repeat*)
And I will raise him up on the last day.

The bread that I will give
Is my/ flesh for the life of the world
And he who/ eats of this bread,
He shall live for ever.

Un/ less you eat
Of the/ flesh of the Son of man
And/ drink of his blood (*repeat*)
You shall/ not have life within you.

I am the resurrection,
I am the life.
He who be/ lieves in me,
Even if he die,
He shall live for ever.

Yes/ Lord, we believe
That/ you are the Christ,
The / Son of God
Who has come
In/ to the world.

61 Anon.
SLW **64**

Oh, the blood of Jesus, (*3 times*)
It washes white as snow.

Oh, the word of Jesus,
It cleanses white as snow.

Oh, the love of Jesus,
It makes his body whole.

62 Sankey
SLW **65**

At the cross, at the cross
    where I first saw the light,
And the burden of my heart rolled away,
It was there by faith I received my sight,
And now I am happy all the day.

63 Anon.
SLW **66**

A new commandment I give unto you,
   that you love one another,
     as I have loved you,
   that you love one another,
     as I have loved you.
By this shall all men know
    you are my disciples
   if you have love one to another.
By this shall all men know
    you are my disciples
   if you have love one to another.

64 Robert Stamps
SLW **67**

O welcome, all ye noble saints of old
As now before your very eyes unfold
The wonders all so long ago foretold:
   God and man at table are sat down.

Elders, martyrs, all are falling down,
Prophets, patriarchs are gathering round.
What angels longed to see
   now man has found.
   God and man at table are sat down.

Who is this who spreads the victory feast?
Who is this who makes our warring cease?
Jesus, risen Saviour, Prince of Peace.
   God and man at table are sat down.

Beggars, lame and harlots also here;
Repentant publicans are drawing near,
Wayward sons come home without a fear,
   God and man at table are sat down.

Worship in the presence of the Lord
With joyful songs and hearts in one accord,
And let our host at table be adored.
   God and man at table are sat down.

When at last this earth shall pass away,
When Jesus and his bride are one to stay,
The feast of love is just begun that day,
   God and man at table are sat down.

65 Tr. Edward Caswall
SLW **68**

Glory be to Jesus,
   Who in bitter pains
Poured for me the life-blood
   From his sacred veins!

Grace and life eternal
   In that blood I find,
Blest be his compassion
   Infinitely kind!

Blest through endless ages
   Be the precious stream
Which from sin and sorrow
   Doth the world redeem!

Oft as earth exulting
   Wafts its praise on high,
Angel-hosts rejoicing,
   Make their glad reply.

Lift ye then your voices;
   Swell the mighty flood;
Louder still and louder
   Praise the precious blood.

66 Ed. Baggett
SLW **69**

Refrain
We really want to thank you, Lord.
We really want to bless your name.
Hallelujah! Jesus is our king!

We thank you, Lord, for your gift to us,
   Your life so rich beyond compare,
The gift of your body here on earth
   Of which we sing and share.

We thank you, Lord, for our life together,
　To live and move in the love of Christ,
Tenderness which sets us free
　To serve you with our lives.

67　Anon.　SLW 70

This is my commandment
　that you love one another,
That your joy may be full.
This is my commandment
　that you love one another,
That your joy may be full
That your joy may be full,
That your joy may be full;
This is my commandment
　that you love one another
That your joy may be full.

68　H. W. Baker　SLW 71

The king of love my shepherd is,
　Whose goodness faileth never;
I nothing lack if I am his,
　And he is mine for ever.

Where streams of living water flow,
　My ransomed soul he leadeth,
And where the verdant pastures grow,
　With food celestial feedeth.

Perverse and foolish oft I strayed,
　But yet in love he sought me,
And on his shoulder gently laid,
　And home, rejoicing, brought me.

In death's dark vale I fear no ill
　With thee, dear Lord, beside me;
Thy rod and staff my comfort still,
　Thy cross before to guide me.

Thou spread'st a table in my sight;
　Thy unction grace bestoweth;
And O what transport of delight
　From thy pure chalice floweth!

And so through all the length of days
　Thy goodness faileth never:
Good shepherd, may I sing thy praise
　Within thy house for ever.

69　John Newton　SLW 72

Glorious things of thee are spoken,
　Zion, city of our God.
He whose word cannot be broken,
　Formed thee for his own abode:
On the rock of ages founded,
　What can shake thy sure repose?
With salvation's walls surrounded,
　Thou may'st smile at all thy foes.

See the streams of living waters,
　Springing from eternal love,
Well supply thy sons and daughters,
　And all fear of want remove:
Who can faint while such a river
　Ever flows their thirst to assuage?
Grace which like the Lord, the giver,
　Ever flows from age to age.

Round each habitation hovering,
　See the cloud and fire appear!
For a glory and a covering
　Showing that the Lord is near:
He who gives them daily manna,
　He who listens when they cry:
Let him hear the loud hosanna,
　Rising to his throne on high.

Saviour, since of Zion's city
　I through grace a member am,
Let the world deride or pity,
　I will glory in thy name;
Fading is the worldling's pleasure,
　All his boasted pomp and show;
Solid joys and lasting treasure
　None but Zion's children know.

Blest inhabitants of Zion;
　Washed in the Redeemer's blood!
Jesus, whom their souls rely on,
　Makes them kings and priests to God.
'Tis his love his people raises
　Over self to reign as kings:
And as priests, his solemn praises
　Each for a thank-offering brings.

70　Diane Davis　SLW 74

God has called [name],
　he will not fail [him/her].
God has called [name],
　he will not fail [him/her].
God has called [name],
　he will not fail [him/her],
So trust in God and obey him.

God has called you, he will not fail you.
So trust in God and obey him.

God has called us, we will not fail him.
So trust in God and obey him.

71
John Rippon
SLW 75

How firm a foundation, ye saints of the Lord,
   Is laid for your faith in his excellent word!
What more can he say
   than to you he hath said,
To you that for refuge to Jesus have fled?

'Fear not, I am with thee; O be not dismayed!
   For I am thy God, and will still give thee aid;
I'll strengthen thee, help thee,
   and cause thee to stand,
Upheld by my righteous, omnipotent hand.

'When through the deep waters
   I call thee to go,
The rivers of woe shall not thee overflow;
For I will be with thee, thy troubles to bless,
   And sanctify to thee thy deepest distress.

'When through fiery trials
   thy pathway shall lie,
My grace, all-sufficient, shall be thy suppy;
The flame shall not hurt thee; I only design
   Thy dross to consume,
   and thy gold to refine.

'The soul that to Jesus has fled for repose,
   I will not, I will not desert to his foes;
That soul, though all hell
   shall endeavour to shake,
I'll never, no never, no never forsake.'

72
Anon.
SLW 76

The fullness of the Godhead bodily
   Dwelleth in my Lord.
The fullness of the Godhead bodily
   Dwelleth in my Lord.
The fullness of the Godhead bodily
   Dwelleth in my Lord
And we are complete in him.

Refrain
Complete, complete,
   Complete in him,
We are complete in him.

It's not by works of righteousness
   But by his grace alone . . .
That we are complete in him.

There's nothing more that I can do
   For Jesus did it all . . .
And we are complete in him.

73
Arr. Betty Pulkingham
SLW 77

Jesus gave her water
That was not from the well,
Gave her living water
And sent her forth to tell:
She went away singing,
And came back bringing
Others for the water
That was not from the well.

Drinking at the springs of living water,
Happy now am I, my soul is satisfied,
Drinking at the springs of living water,
What a wonderful and bounteous supply.

Spring up, O well, within my soul.
Spring up, O well, and overflow;
Spring up, O well, flow out through me.
Spring up, O well, set others free.

There's a river of life flowing out through me,
   It makes the lame to walk
      and the blind to see,
Opens prison doors, sets the captives free,
   There's a river of life flowing out
      through me.

There's a fountain flowing
      from the Saviour's side,
All my sins forgiven in that precious tide.
Jesus paid the price when for me he died.
   There's a fountain flowing
      from the Saviour's side.

There's a risen Saviour at the Father's throne,
   Ever interceding for his very own,
Pouring down the blessings that are his alone.
   There's a risen Saviour at the Father's
      throne.

There's a holy comforter
   who's sent from heaven,
All the glorious gifts are his,
   and have been given,
He'll/show us more of Jesus
   'til the veil is riven.
There's a holy comforter
   who's sent from heaven.

There's a land of rest that we may enter now,
    Freed from all our works
        and freed from Satan's power,
Just /resting in the Lord each moment
        and each hour.
    There's a land of rest
        that we may enter now.

There's a full salvation
    wrought for you and me,
From /faith to faith and /glory
    to glory e/ternally,
O/Lord, just take this life and let me live
    for thee.
    There's a full salvation
        wrought for you and me.

74   Paul Smith   SLW 78

I have decided to follow Jesus.
I have decided to follow Jesus.
I have decided to follow Jesus.
    No turning back, no turning back.

The world behind me, the cross before me.
    No turning back, no turning back.

Tho' none go with me, still I will follow.
    No turning back, no turning back.

Where Jesus leads me, I'll surely follow.
    No turning back, no turning back.

Sing glory, glory and hallelujah.
    No turning back, no turning back.

75   Christopher Wordsworth   SLW 79

See the conqueror mounts in triumph,
See the King in royal state,
Riding on the clouds, his chariot,
To his heavenly palace gate!
    Hark! the choirs of angel voices
    Joyful alleluias sing.
    And the portals high are lifted
    To receive their heavenly King.

He who on the cross did suffer,
He who from the grave arose,
He has vanquished sin and Satan:
He by death has spoiled his foes.
    While he lifts his hands in blessing,
    He is parted from his friends;
    While their eager eyes behold him,
    He upon the clouds ascends.

Thou hast raised our human nature
On the clouds to God's right hand:
There we sit in heavenly places,
There with thee in glory stand.
    Jesus reigns, adored by angels;
    Man with God is on the throne;
    Mighty Lord, in thine ascension,
    We by faith behold our own.

76   John Blackwell and Martin Madan   SLW 80

Hail, thou once despised Jesus!
Hail, thou Galilean King!
Thou didst suffer to release us;
Thou didst free salvation bring.
    Hail, thou universal Saviour,
    Bearer of our sin and shame.
    By thy merit we find favour:
    Life is given through thy name.

Paschal Lamb, by God appointed,
All our sins on thee were laid:
By almighty love anointed,
Thou hast full atonement made.
    All thy people are forgiven
    Through the virtue of thy blood:
    Opened is the gate of heaven,
    Peace is made 'twixt man and God.

Jesus, hail! enthroned in glory,
There for ever to abide;
All the heavenly hosts adore thee,
Seated at thy Father's side.
    There for sinners thou art pleading:
    There thou dost our place prepare;
    Ever for us interceding,
    Till in glory we appear.

Worship, honour, power, and blessing
Thou art worthy to receive:
Highest praises, without ceasing,
Meet it is for us to give.
    Help, ye bright angelic spirits,
    Bring your sweetest, noblest lays;
    Help to sing our Saviour's merits,
    Help to chant Emmanuel's praise!

77   Anon.   SLW 81

He signed my deed with his atoning blood,
He ever lives to make his promise good.
Though all the hosts of hell march in
    to make a second claim,
They'll all march out at the mention
    of his name. (*3 times*)

78
David J. Mansell
SLW 82

'Jesus is Lord!' Creation's voice proclaims it,
For by his power each tree and flower
   was planned and made.
'Jesus is Lord!' The universe declares it.
Sun, moon and stars in heaven cry
   'Jesus is Lord!'

Refrain
Jesus is Lord! Jesus is Lord!
Praise him with 'Hallelujahs' for Jesus is Lord!

Jesus is Lord! Yet from his throne eternal
In flesh he came to die in pain
   on Calvary's tree.
Jesus is Lord! From him all life proceeding,
Yet gave his life a ransom thus setting us free.

Jesus is Lord! O'er sin the mighty conqueror,
From death he rose and all his foes
   shall own his name.
Jesus is Lord! God sends his Holy Spirit
To show by works of power that Jesus is Lord.

79
Anon.
SLW 83

The joy of the Lord is my strength. (*4 times*)

Refrain
A-ha-ha-ha ... *Lines 1–3*
The joy of the Lord is my strength.

If you want joy you must sing for it,
If you want joy you must shout for it;
If you want joy you must jump for it.
The joy of the Lord is my strength.

The word of faith is nigh thee,
   even in thy mouth. (*3 times*)
The joy of the Lord is my strength.

80
Jacob Krieger
SLW 84

I heard the Lord
   Call my name,
Listen close,
   You'll hear the same.
I heard the Lord
   Call my name,
Listen close,
   You'll hear the same.

I heard the Lord
   Call my name,
Listen close,
   You'll hear the same.
Take his hand,
We are glory bound.

His word is love,
   Love's his word,
That's the message
   That I heard.
Take his hand,
We are glory bound.

Place your hand in his and
   You will know
He will show you
   Where to go.

I felt his love
   From above
Settle on me
   Like a dove.
Take his hand,
We are glory bound.

And to the Father
   All your days
With the Son
   And Spirit praise.
Take his hand,
We are glory bound.

Place your hand in his and
   You will know,
He will show you
   Where to go.

Repeat first verse.

81
Charles Wesley
SLW 85

And can it be that I should gain
   An interest in the Saviour's blood?
Died he for me, who caused his pain?
   For me, who him to death pursued?
Amazing love! how can it be
That thou, my God, shouldst die for me?

'Tis mystery all! th'immortal dies!
   Who can explore his strange design?
In vain the firstborn seraph tries
   To sound the depths of love divine!
'Tis mercy all! let earth adore,
Let angel minds inquire no more.

He left his father's throne above,
  So free, so infinite his grace;
Emptied himself of all but love,
  And bled for Adam's helpless race;
'Tis mercy all, immense and free;
For, O my God, it found out me.

Long my imprisoned spirit lay
  Fast bound in sin and nature's night;
Thine eye diffused a quickening ray,
  I woke, the dungeon flamed with light;
My chains fell off, my heart was free;
I rose, went forth, and followed thee.

No condemnation now I dread;
  Jesus and all in him, is mine!
Alive in him, my living head,
  And clothed in righteousness divine,
Bold I approach the eternal throne,
And claim the crown, through Christ my own.

82   Mimi Farra
       SLW **86**

Refrain
Alleluia! Alleluia!
Alleluia, sons of God, arise.
Alleluia! Alleluia! Sons of God,
Arise and follow the Lord.

Come and be clothed in his righteousness;
Come join the band who are called
  by his name.

Look at the world which is bound by sin;
Walk into the midst of it proclaiming my life.

83   Anon.
       SLW **87**

Come and go with me to my Father's house,
  to my Father's house, to my Father's house.
Come and go with me to my Father's house
  where there's joy, joy, joy.

It's not very far to my Father's house . . .

There is room for all in my Father's house . . .

Everything is free in my Father's house . . .

Jesus is the way to my Father's house . . .

Jesus is the light in my Father's house . . .

84   Author unknown
       SLW **88**

Refrain
Ho! everyone that thirsteth,
  come ye to the waters,
and he that hath no money, come ye,
  buy and eat.

Come, buy without money;
  come, buy without price.
Come, buy milk and honey
  from Jesus Christ.

Wherefore do you spend money
  for that which is not bread;
and your labour for that which satis-
-fieth not?

Hearken unto me and
  eat that which is good;
let your soul delight itself in
  fatness, fatness, fatness.

85   Anon.
       SLW **89**

Take my hand and follow me
To see the sea walker, the blind man healer,
The leper-cleansing man of Galilee.
He's the soul-saver, the one who set me free,
Take my hand and follow me.

86   Patrick Appleford
       SLW **90**

O Lord, all the world belongs to you,
And you are always making all things new.
What is wrong you forgive,
  and the new life you give
Is what's turning the world upside down.

The world's only loving to its friends,
But your way of loving never ends;
Loving enemies too, and this loving with you
Is what's turning the world upside down.

This world lives divided and apart;
You draw men together and we start
In your body to see that in fellowship we
Can be turning the world upside down.

The world wants the wealth to live in state,
But you show a new way to be great:
Like a servant you came,
  and if we do the same,
We'll be turning the world upside down.

O Lord, all the world belongs to you,
And you are always making all things new,
Send your Spirit on all in your Church
   whom you call
To be turning the world upside down.

87   Anon.   SLW 91

Peace is flowing like a river,
Flowing out through you and me,
Spreading out into the desert,
Setting all the captives free.

88   Arthur Ainger   SLW 92

God is working his purpose out
As year succeeds to year:
God is working his purpose out,
And the time is drawing near;
Nearer and nearer draws the time;
The time that shall surely be,
When the earth shall be filled
   with the glory of God
As the waters cover the sea.

From utmost east to utmost west.
Where'er man's foot hath trod,
By the mouth of many messengers
Goes forth the voice of God;
Give ear to me, ye continents,
Ye isles, give ear to me,
That the earth may be filled
   with the glory of God
As the waters cover the sea.

March we forth in the strength of God,
With the banner of Christ unfurled,
That the light of the glorious gospel of truth
May shine throughout the world;
Fight we the fight with sorrow and sin
To set their captives free,
That the earth may be filled
   with the glory of God
As the waters cover the sea.

All we can do is nothing worth
Unless God blesses the deed;
Vainly we hope for the harvest tide
Till God gives life to the seed;
Yet nearer and nearer draws the time,
The time that shall surely be,
When the earth shall be filled
   with the glory of God
As the waters cover the sea.

89   Alan Dale   SLW 93

God's Spirit is in my heart,
He has called me and set me apart.
This is what I have to do,
   What I have to do:

Refrain
He sent me to give the good news to the poor,
   Tell prisoners that they are prisoners
      no more;
Tell blind people that they can see,
   And set the down-trodden free.
And go tell everyone the news that the
      kingdom of God has come,
   And go tell everyone the news
      that God's kingdom has come.

Just as the Father sent me
   So I'm sending you out to be
My witness throughout the world,
   The whole of the world.

Don't carry a load in your pack,
   You don't need two shirts on your back,
A workman can earn his own keep,
   Can earn his own keep.

Don't worry what you have to say,
   Don't worry because on that day
God's Spirit will speak in your heart,
   Will speak in your heart.

90   Mary Ann Thompson   SLW 94

O Zion, haste, thy mission high fulfilling,
   To tell to all the world that God is light;
That he who made all nations is not willing
   One soul should perish,
      lost in shades of night:

Refrain
Publish glad tidings: tidings of peace,
   Tidings of Jesus, redemption and release.

Proclaim to every people, tongue, and nation
   That God, in whom they live and move,
      is love;
Tell how he stooped to save his lost creation,
   And died on earth that man might
      live above.

Give of thy sons to bear the message glorious;
   Give of thy wealth to speed them
      on their way;

CELEBRATION

Pour out thy soul for them
   in prayer victorious
Till God shall bring his kingdom's
   joyful day.

He comes again! O Zion, ere thou meet him,
  Make known to every heart
    his saving grace;
Let none whom he hath ransomed fail
   to greet him,
Through thy neglect, unfit to see his face.

91
W. F. Jabusch
SLW **95**

Refrain
God has spoken to his people, hallelujah!
And his words are words of wisdom,
   hallelujah!

Open your ears, O Christian people,
  Open your ears and hear good news.
Open your hearts, O royal priesthood,
  God has come to you.

He who has ears to hear his message,
  He who has ears, then let him hear.
He who would learn the way of wisdom,
  Let him hear God's word.

Israel comes to greet the Saviour;
  Judah is glad to see his day.
From east and west the peoples travel,
  He will show the way.

92
J. E. Seddon
SLW **96**

Go forth and tell! O Church of God awake!
  God's saving news to all the nations take.
Proclaim Christ Jesus, Saviour, Lord,
   and King,
That all the world his worthy praise
   may sing.

Go forth and tell! God's love embraces all:
  He will in grace respond to all who call.
How shall they call if they have never heard
  The gracious invitation of his word?

Go forth and tell! Men still in darkness lie:
  In wealth or want, in sin they live and die.
Give us, O Lord, concern of heart and mind,
  A love like thine which cares for all mankind.

Go forth and tell! The doors are open wide:
  Share God's good gifts with men so long
   denied.
Live out your life as Christ, your Lord, shall
   choose,
  Your ransomed powers for his sole
   glory use.

Go forth and tell! O Church of God, arise:
  Go in the strength which Christ your
   Lord supplies.
Go, till all nations his great name adore
  And serve him Lord and King for evermore.

93
Jane Trigg
SLW **97**

Refrain
Joy in the Lord,
O be joyful in the Lord,
All ye lands.

Serve the Lord with gladness.
Come before him with a song.

Be sure the Lord is God.
He hath made us, we are his.

O go into his courts
With thanksgiving and praise.

Be thankful unto him,
And speak good of his name.

The Lord is gracious,
Merciful for evermore.

94
Author unknown
SLW **98**

Refrain
Behold how good and how pleasant it is
  for brethren to dwell together in unity.

It is like the precious ointment upon the head
  that ran down upon the beard,
   even Aaron's beard,
that ran down to the skirts of his garments;

As the dew of Hermon and as the dew
  that descended upon the mountain of Zion,
for there the Lord commanded blessing.

For there the Lord commanded,
  commanded the blessing,
even life for evermore.

95
Author unknown
SLW 99

When the Lord restored the fortunes of Zion,
   we were like those who dream.
Then our mouths were filled with laughter,
   and our tongues with shouts of joy!

Refrain
The Lord has done great things for us
   and we are glad.

Then they said among the nations,
   'The Lord has done great things for us.'

Restore our fortunes, O Lord,
   as the water courses in the Negeb.
May those who sow in tears,
   reap with shouts of joy!

He that goes forth weeping
   bearing the seed for sowing,
shall come home with shouts of joy,
   bringing his sheaves with him.

96
Mimi Farra
SLW 100

Refrain
The Lord hath put a new song in my mouth,
   in my mouth, in my mouth.
The Lord hath put a new song in my mouth,
   even praise unto our God.

And many shall see it and fear and trust,
   fear and trust, fear and trust,
And many shall see it and fear and trust,
   and shall trust in the Lord.

I delight to do thy will, oh God,
   thy will, oh God, thy will, oh God,
I delight to do thy will, oh God.
   Thy law is within my heart.

I have not hid thy righteousness
   within my heart,
   within my heart, within my heart.
I have not hid thy righteousness
   within my heart.
I have declared thy salvation.

I've not concealed thy loving kindness
   and thy truth,
   and thy truth, and thy truth,
I've not concealed thy loving kindness
   and thy truth,
   from the great congregation.

So let thy loving kindness and thy truth,
   and thy truth, and thy truth,
so let thy loving kindness and thy truth
   continually preserve me.

Let all those that seek thee rejoice and be glad,
   rejoice and be glad, rejoice and be glad.
Let all those that seek thee rejoice and be glad
   rejoice and be glad in thee.

Refrain
The Lord hath put a new song in my mouth,
   in my mouth, in my mouth.
The Lord hath put a new song in my mouth,
   even praise unto our God.

97
Mike Fitzgerald
SLW 101

Refrain
As a doe longs for running streams,
so longs my soul for you, my God.

My soul is thirsting for the God of life;
   when shall I see him face to face?
I have no food but tears day and night;
   and men say, 'Where is your God?'

I remember and my soul melts within.
   I'm on my way to the house of God,
among cries of joy and praise;
   place your trust in God.

Why so downcast, O my soul?
   Why do you sigh so deep within?
Place your hope in the God of life.
   I shall praise him again.

When I find my soul downcast within,
   I think of you, O mount Zion.
Deep calls to deep as your waters roar;
   over me all your waves pour.

98
Jessie Seymour Irvine
SLW 102

The Lord's my shepherd, I'll not want;
   He makes me down to lie
In pastures green; he leadeth me
   The quiet waters by.

My soul he doth restore again;
   And me to walk doth make
Within the paths of righteousness,
   E'en for his own name's sake.

Yea, though I walk in death's dark vale,
   Yet will I fear none ill:
For thou art with me; and thy rod
   And staff me comfort still.

My table thou hast furnished
   In presence of my foes;
My head thou dost with oil anoint,
   And my cup overflows.

Goodness and mercy all my life
   Shall surely follow me:
And in God's house for evermore
   My dwelling-place shall be.

99   Timothy Dudley-Smith   SLW 103

Sing a new song to the Lord,
   He to whom wonders belong!
Rejoice in his triumph and tell of his power,
   O sing to the Lord a new song!

Now to the ends of the earth
   See his salvation is shown!
And still he remembers his mercy and truth,
   Unchanging in love to his own.

Sing a new song and rejoice,
   Publish his praises abroad!
Let voices in chorus, with trumpet and horn,
   Resound for the joy of the Lord!

Join with the hills and the sea
   Thunders of praise to prolong!
In judgement and justice
   he comes to the earth,
   O sing to the Lord a new song!

100   Author unknown   SLW 104

Refrain
Bless thou the Lord, O my soul, (*3 times*)
and forget not all his benefits.

Who forgiveth all thine iniquities,
   who healeth all thy diseases.

Who redeemeth thy life from destruction,
   who crowneth thee with loving kindness.

The Lord is merciful and gracious,
   slow to anger and plenteous in mercy.

For as the heaven is high above the earth,
   so great his mercy toward them
     that fear him.

Like as a father pitieth his children,
   so the Lord pitieth them that fear him.

101   Betty Pulkingham   SLW 105

Refrain
I rejoiced when I heard them say,
   'Let us go to God's house today!'
I rejoiced when I heard them say,
   'Let us go to God's house.'

And now our feet are standing,
   standing within thy gates.
O Jerusalem.

Jerusalem is built as a city,
   it is there that the tribes go up,
the tribes of the Lord.

For the peace of Jerusalem pray,
   peace be to your homes,
Peace to your homes alway.

For love of my brethren and friends,
   for love of the house of the Lord,
I will say, 'Peace, peace upon you.'

After final refrain:
   Let us go to God's house.

102   Brian Howard   SLW 106

If I were a butterfly,
   I'd thank you, Lord, for giving me wings.
And if I were a robin in a tree,
   I'd thank you, Lord, that I could sing.
And if I were a fish in the sea,
   I'd wiggle my tail and I'd giggle with glee,
But I just thank you, Father,
   for making me 'me'.

Refrain
For you gave me a heart
   and you gave me a smile.
You gave me Jesus
   and you made me your child.
And I just thank you, Father,
   for making me 'me'.

103 John Franklin (Age 12)
SLW **107**

Refrain
Jesus, Jesus is my Lord;
Always obey what Jesus says.

That's the way to lay down your life,
  always obey what Jesus says.
The ones who come for Jesus' life,
  always obey what Jesus says.

He rewards you, making you free,
  always . . .
And then you have power over the enemy,
  always . . .

He has given his Spirit to you,
  always . . .
So keep his words and he will keep you,
  always . . .

If I were an elephant,
  I'd thank you, Lord, by raising my trunk,
And if I were a kangaroo,
  You know I'd hop right up to you.
And if I were an octopus,
  I'd thank you, Lord, for my fine looks,
But I just thank you, Father,
  for making me 'me'.

If I were a wiggily worm,
  I'd thank you, Lord, that I could squirm.
And if I were a billy goat
  I'd thank you Lord for my strong throat,
And if I were a fuzzy-wuzzy bear,
  I'd thank you, Lord,
    for my fuzzy-wuzzy hair,
But I just thank you, Father,
  for making me 'me'.

104 Anon.
SLW **108**

The Lord is my shepherd,
  I'll follow him alway.
He leads me by still waters,
  I'll follow him alway.
Alway, alway,
  I'll follow him alway.
Alway, alway,
  I'll follow him alway.

105 Refrain: F. Whitfield
SLW **109**

Q **Hey, [name], do you love Jesus?**
A   Yes, I love Jesus.
Q   Are you sure you love Jesus?
A   Yes, I'm sure I love Jesus.
Q   Tell me, why do you love Jesus?
A   This is why I love Jesus,
All Because he first loved me,
  Yes, I love him,
  This is why I love him;

Refrain
Oh, how I love Jesus,
Oh, how I love Jesus,
Oh, how I love Jesus,
  Because he first loved me.
All Yes, I love him, this is why I love him . . .

106 Elizabeth Syré
SLW **110**

Refrain
Sing, sing, praise and sing!
Honour God for everything.
Glory to the highest king.
Sing and praise and sing!

Clap your hands, lift your voice,
Praise the Lord and rejoice!

Full of joy, full of rest,
In our Lord we are blessed.

Are you weak? Never mind!
Come and sing, 'God is kind!'

Love and peace is so near.
Praise the Lord! God can hear!

Cymbal, harp, violin,
Angels, priests, all join in.

107 Betty Pulkingham
SLW **111**

If the eye say to the hand,
  'I have no need of thee.'
Or the head to the feet,
  'I have no need of you.'
Well, oh how can we write or hold a thimble?
  How can we walk or run so nimble?
How can the body be complete without feet?
  How can the body be complete?

If the foot shall say, 'Because I'm not the hand,
   I don't feel like a handsome part.'
Well, oh what does it matter
      to be first or to be latter?
   God has made the body whole
      and formed each part,
   God has made the body whole
      and formed each part.

If the ear shall say, 'Because I'm not the eye,
   I don't seem to see things very clearly.'
Well, oh where were the hearing,
      and oh where were the smelling
   If the whole body were one single eye,
   If the whole body were one eye.

One single 'I', it cannot be a body.
   One single 'you' a body? 'Nay!'
Oh, God hath set the members,
   They are many, many members,
Yet one body as it pleased him are they.
   Yet one body as it pleased him are they.

108 David Pulkingham (age 4)
        SLW 112

We love the Lord,
   Our neighbours and ourselves.
We open our eyes,
   We see him everywhere.
We love the Lord,
   Who died on the cross.
We love the Lord
   To love each other too.
We open our eyes,
   We see Jesus Christ;
He looks down at us,
   We look up at him.
We trust in him
   Eternally.

109 Diane Davis
        SLW 113

Thank you, Lord, for this fine day, (*3 times*)
Right where we are.

Refrain
Alleluia, praise the Lord.
Alleluia, praise the Lord.
Alleluia, praise the Lord,
Right where we are.

Thank you, Lord, for loving us.

Thank you, Lord, for giving us peace.

Thank you, Lord, for setting us free.

Thank you, Lord, for games to play.

110 Paul Mazak (age 4)
        SLW 114

Jesus is a friend of mine,
   Praise him.
Jesus is a friend of mine,
   Praise him.
Praise him, praise him.
Jesus is a friend of mine,
   Praise him.

Jesus died to set us free,
   Praise him.

He gave us the victory,
   Praise him.

Jesus is the King of kings,
   Praise him.

111 Miriam Therese Winter
        SLW 115

Refrain
I cannot come.
   I cannot come to the banquet,
      don't trouble me now.
   I have married a wife,
      I have bought me a cow.
   I have fields and commitments
      that cost a pretty sum.
      Pray, hold me excused, I cannot come.

A certain man held a feast
      on his fine estate in town,
He laid a festive table
      and wore a wedding gown.
He sent invitations to his neighbours
      far and wide,
But when the meal was ready,
      each of them replied:

The master rose up in anger,
      called his servants by name,
Said: 'Go into the town, fetch the blind
      and the lame,
Fetch the peasant and the pauper,
      for this I have willed,
My banquet must be crowded,
      and my table must be filled.'

When all the poor had assembled,
    there was still room to spare,
So the master demanded:
    'Go search everywhere,
To the highways and the byways,
    and force them to come in.
My table must be filled before the banquet
    can begin.'

Now God has written a lesson
    for the rest of mankind;
If we're slow in responding,
    he may leave us behind.
He's preparing a banquet for that great
    and glorious day.
When the Lord and Master calls us,
    be certain not to say:

112   Betty Pulkingham   SLW 116

Refrain
Wake up! Wake up! It's time to rise and sing
    the praise of Jesus,
    Allelu, alleluia.
It's time to rise, to sing, to shout,
    to bring him all your heart.
He'll do the bigger part, if you will only
    make a start.

In the days of Noah's family,
    The people didn't know what the score was
        eternally.
They ate, and drank, got married and then
    Their sons and their daughters did the same
        things again.

John came baptising in the wilderness;
    Preaching to those
        who their sins confessed.
But to those who came for strife and
    debate, he said,
    'Who told you to come here,
        you tribe of snakes!'

When Jesus came to John in the wilderness;
    John said, 'I should be the one to come
        to you, I must confess!
For I baptise with water at the most,
    But you will baptise with the Holy Ghost!'

Jesus told a story of ten maidens fair;
    Five were wise and ready,
        five did not prepare.
Those girls had lamps, but oh, dear me!
    They had no oil to light them
        so that they could see.

What good is a lamp without any oil?
    What good is our life if we struggle and toil,
But cannot see God's kingdom here,
    And live the loving life of his Son so dear?

113   Charles Coffin (Tr. John Chandler)   SLW 117

On Jordan's bank the Baptist's cry
    Announces that the Lord is nigh;
Awake and hearken, for he brings
    Glad tidings of the King of kings.

Then cleansed be every breast from sin;
    Make straight the way for God within,
And let each heart prepare a home
    Where such a mighty guest may come.

For thou art our salvation, Lord,
    Our refuge, and our great reward;
Without thy grace we waste away
    Like flowers that wither and decay.

To heal the sick stretch out thine hand,
    And bid the fallen sinner stand;
Shine forth, and let thy light restore
    Earth's own true loveliness once more.

All praise, eternal Son, to thee,
    Whose advent doth thy people free;
Whom with the Father we adore
    And Holy Ghost for evermore.

114   Michael Perry   SLW 118

See him a-lying on a bed of straw;
    Draughty stable with an open door,
Mary cradling the babe she bore;
    The prince of glory is his name.

Refrain
Oh, now carry me to Bethlehem
    To see the Lord appear to men;
Just as poor as was the stable then,
    The prince of glory when he came.

Star of silver sweep across the skies,
    Show where Jesus in the manger lies.
Shepherds swiftly from your stupor rise
    To see the Saviour of the world.

Angels, sing again the song you sang,
    Bring God's glory to the heart of man;
Sing that Bethl'hem's little baby can
    Be salvation to the soul.

Mine are riches from thy poverty,
    From thine innocence, eternity;
Mine, forgiveness by thy death for me,
    Child of sorrow for my joy.

Teach, O teach us, holy child,
    By thy face so meek and mild,
Teach us to resemble thee
    In thy sweet humility.

115   Mimi Farra   SLW 119

Refrain
Oh, Mary don't you weep,
And Mary don't you cry.

Oh, little baby Jesus,
    Baby Jesus is gonna die, but . . .

Baby Jesus is gonna die,
    Gonna die that we might live for ever.

Oh, sing glory hallelujah,
    Glory, glory baby Jesus.

116   Edward Caswall   SLW 120

See amid the winter's snow,
    Born for us on earth below
See the tender Lamb appears,
    Promised from eternal years.

Refrain
Hail, thou ever-blessed morn!
Hail redemption's happy dawn!
Sing through all Jerusalem:
Christ is born in Bethlehem.

Lo, within a manger lies
    He who built the starry skies,
He who throned in height sublime,
    Sits amid the cherubim.

Say, ye holy shepherds, say,
    What your joyful news today;
Wherefore have ye left your sheep
    On the lonely mountain steep?

'As we watched at dead of night,
    Lo, we saw a wondrous light:
Angels, singing peace on earth,
    Told us of the Saviour's birth.

Sacred infant, all divine,
    What a tender love was thine,
Thus to come from highest bliss
    Down to such a world as this!

117   North American spiritual   SLW 121

Refrain
Go tell it on the mountain,
    Over the hills and everywhere.
Go tell it on the mountain
    That Jesus Christ is born.

While shepherds kept their watching
    O'er silent flocks by night,
Behold throughout the heavens
    There shone a holy light.

The shepherds feared and trembled
    When lo, above the earth
Rang out the angel chorus
    That hailed the Saviour's birth.

Down in a lowly manger
    Our humble Christ was born,
And God sent us salvation
    That blessed Christmas morn.

When I was a seeker,
    I sought both night and day;
I asked the Lord to help me,
    And he showed me the way.

He made me a watchman
    Upon the city wall,
And if I am a Christian,
    I am the least of all.

118   Shirley Lewis Brown   SLW 122

Let your light shine,
    Let your light shine,
Let your light shine before men,
That they may see,
    May see your good works,
And glorify the Father,
    The Father,
The Father who is in heaven.

Once there was darkness,
    Once there was darkness,
Once there was darkness upon earth.
Then God sent Jesus,
    Then God sent Jesus

To light the way, the pathway,
    The pathway,
The pathway back to God.

What did he tell us?
    What did he tell us?
What did he tell us we should do?
He said to love God,
    To love your neighbour,
And serve him; let your light shine,
    Let your light shine,
Let your light shine before men.

119   Traditional   SLW 123

What wondrous love is this, O my soul,
    O my soul?
What wondrous love is this, O my soul?
What wondrous love is this that caused
    the Lord of bliss
To bear the dreadful curse for my soul,
    for my soul,
To bear the dreadful curse for my soul.

When I was sinking down, sinking down,
    sinking down,
When I was sinking down, sinking down,
When I was sinking down beneath God's
    righteous frown,
Christ laid aside his crown for my soul,
    for my soul,
Christ laid aside his crown for my soul.

To God and to the Lamb I will sing, I will sing,
To God and to the Lamb I will sing.
To God and to the Lamb who is the great I AM,
While thousands join the theme, I will sing,
    I will sing,
While thousands join the theme, I will sing.

And when from death I'm free, I'll sing on,
    I'll sing on,
And when from death I'm free, I'll sing on.
And when from death I'm free, I'll sing
    and joyful be,
And through eternity I'll sing on, I'll sing on,
And through eternity I'll sing on.

120   W. F. Jabusch   SLW 124

Refrain
The King of glory comes,
The nation rejoices.
Open the gates before him,
Lift up your voices.

Who is the King of glory; how shall we
    call him?
He is Emmanuel, the promised of ages.

In all of Galilee, in city or village,
He goes among his people curing their illness.

Sing then of David's son, our Saviour
    and brother;
In all of Galilee was never another.

He gave his life for us, the pledge of salvation.
He took upon himself the sins of the nation.

He conquered sin and death; he truly
    has risen,
And he will share with us his heavenly vision.

121   Shirley Lewis Brown   SLW 125

Refrain
Put on the apron of humility;
Serve your brother, wash his feet,
That he may walk in the way of the Lord,
Refreshed, refreshed.

At the last supper with his disciples Jesus rose
    from the table,
took a towel and a basin of water and stooped
    to wash their feet.

When Jesus knelt before him, Peter said,
    'Lord, do you wash my feet?'
Jesus answered, 'Now you don't understand,
    but later on you will.'
Still protesting, Peter said, 'Lord,
    you must never wash my feet.'
Jesus answered, 'If I don't wash you,
    you have no part of me.'

Then said Peter, 'Lord, not only my feet,
    but also my hands and my head.'
Jesus answered, 'He who has washed need
    only wash his feet.'

Then said Jesus, 'Do you know what it is
    that I have done?
You call me your master and Lord,
    and you speak the truth, for so I am.
If I then, your master and Lord,
    have stooped to wash your feet,
So ought you men also to wash the feet
    of one another.

'No man is greater than his master, no
    messenger than he who sent him.
If you men know these things then happy are
    you if you do them.'

CELEBRATION

122 North American spiritual
SLW **126**

Were you there when they crucified my Lord?
Oh! Sometimes it causes me to tremble,
   tremble, tremble.
Were you there when they crucified my Lord?

Were you there when they nailed him
   to the tree?
Oh! Sometimes it causes me to tremble,
   tremble, tremble.
Were you there when they nailed him
   to the tree?

Were you there when they laid him
   in the tomb?
Oh! Sometimes it causes me to tremble,
   tremble, tremble.
Were you there when they laid him
   in the tomb?

Were you there when he rose up
   from the dead?
Oh! Sometimes it causes me to shout
   'Hallelujah!'
Were you there when he rose up
   from the dead?

123 Edmond Louis Budry (Tr. Richard Birch Hoyle)
SLW **128**

Thine be the glory, risen, conquering Son,
Endless is the victory thou o'er death
   hast won;
Angels in bright raiment
   rolled the stone away,
Kept the folded grave-clothes,
   where thy body lay.

Refrain
Thine be the glory, risen, conquering Son,
Endless is the victory thou o'er death
   hast won!

Lo, Jesus meets us, risen, from the tomb!
Lovingly he greets us, scatters fear
   and gloom;
Let the church with gladness
   hymns of triumph sing,
For her Lord now liveth,
   death hath lost its sting.

No more we doubt thee,
   glorious prince of life;
Life is nought without thee:
   aid us in our strife;
Make us more than conquerors,
   through thy deathless love;
Bring us safe through Jordan
   to thy home above.

124 Charles Wesley, adapted by Betty Pulkingham
SLW **129**

Christ the Lord is risen today:
   Sons of men and angels say,
Hallelujah! Hallelujah! Halle-lujah today!
   Raise your joys and triumphs high:
   Sing, you heavens and you earth reply,
      Hallelujah!

Love's redeeming work is done:
   Fought the fight the battle won;
Hallelujah! Hallelujah! Halle-lujah today!
   Death in vain forbids him rise:
   Christ has opened paradise. Hallelujah!

Lives again our glorious King!
   Where, O death, is now your sting?
Hallelujah! Hallelujah! Halle-lujah today!
   Once he died our souls to save;
   Where is your victory, O grave?
      Hallelujah!

Soar we now where Christ has led
   Following our exalted Head.
Hallelujah! Hallelujah! Halle-lujah today!
   Made like him, like him we rise,
   Ours the cross, the grave, the skies.
      Hallelujah!
Christ the Lord is risen . . . today!

(124) Charles Wesley
SLW **130**

Christ the Lord is risen today: Hallelujah!
   Sons of men and angels say, 'Hallelujah!'
Raise your joys and triumphs high: Hallelujah!
   Sing ye heavens, thou earth reply,
      Hallelujah!

Love's redeeming work is done; Hallelujah!
   Fought the fight, the battle won, Hallelujah!
Death in vain forbids him rise, Hallelujah!
   Christ hath opened paradise, Hallelujah!

Lives again our glorious King! Hallelujah!
   Where, O death, is now thy sting?
      Hallelujah!
Once he died our souls to save, Hallelujah!
   Where thy victory, O grave? Hallelujah!

Soar we now where Christ has led, Hallelujah!
　Following our exalted Head; Hallelujah!
Made like him, like him we rise; Hallelujah!
　Ours the cross, the grave, the skies;
　　Hallelujah!

125 Refrain: Mrs C. H. Morris;
Verses: Betty Pulkingham
SLW 131

Refrain
He will fill your hearts today
　to overflowing,
As the Lord commanded you
　'Bring your vessels not a few,'
He will fill your hearts today to overflowing
　With his Holy Ghost and power.

When the day of Pentecost had come,
　The believers were gathered together,
Were gathered together in one place,
　Of one mind as the Lord had commanded.

Suddenly a noise from the sky,
　Which sounded like a strong wind blowing,
A strong wind blowing by,
　Filled the whole place,
　　the noise kept on growing.

Then they looked up and saw,
　They saw what looked like tongues of fire,
Tongues of fire spreading out,
　To each one, spreading out to all the people.

All of them were filled with the Holy Ghost,
　With the Holy Ghost and power.
They began to speak in other languages,
　In other languages he gave them
　　in that hour!

126 Traditional
SLW 132

Come, Holy Ghost creator blest,
　Vouchsafe within our souls to rest;
Come with thy grace and heavenly aid,
And fill the hearts which thou hast made,
And fill the hearts which thou hast made.

To thee the comforter we cry;
　To thee the gift of God most high;
The fount of life, the fire of love,
　The soul's anointing from above.

The sevenfold gifts of grace are thine,
　O finger of the hand divine.
True promise of the Father thou,
　Who dost the tongue with speech endow.

Thy light to every sense impart,
　And shed thy love in every heart;
Thine own unfailing might supply,
　To strengthen our infirmity.

Drive far away our ghostly foe,
　And thine abiding peace bestow;
If thou be our preventing guide,
　No evil can our steps betide.

127 Jeff Cothran
SLW 133

Planted wheat, within the wheatfields,
　waiting till the summer time is near.
Growing wheat, above the ploughlands,
　showing that the Lord of lords is here.

Refrain
He comes to grow a new creation,
　calling out a holy nation,
　all who will believe, and all who will receive.

Jesus rose, we cannot see him;
　he is seated at the Father's hand.
Yet he walks within his harvest,
　men in love obeying his command.

Jesus Christ is Lord of the harvest.
　Soon in glory he will come again,
Bringing all his holy angels,
　gathering in the ripened sheaves of grain.

FRESH SOUNDS

128 Traditional
FS 1

San-na, san-na-ni-na,
 San-na, san-na, san-na.
San-na, san-na-ni-na,
 San-na, san-na, san-na.

San-na, san-na,
 San-na, san-na-ni-na,
San-na, san-na, san-na.

129 James Montgomery
FS 2

Hail to the Lord's anointed,
 Great David's greater Son!
Hail in the time appointed,
 His reign on earth begun!
He comes to break oppression,
 To set the captive free;
To take away transgression,
 And rule in equity.

He shall come down like showers
 Upon the fruitful earth,
And love, joy, hope, like flowers,
 Spring in his path to birth:
Before him on the mountains
 Shall peace, the herald go;
And righteousness in fountains
 From hill to valley flow.

Kings shall bow down before him,
 And gold and incense bring;
All nations shall adore him,
 His praise all people sing;
For he shall have dominion
 O'er every sea and shore;
His kingdom still increasing,
 A kingdom for evermore.

O'er every foe victorious,
 He on his throne shall rest;
From age to age more glorious,
 All blessing and all-blest:
The tide of time shall never
 His covenant remove;
His name shall stand for ever,
 His changeless name of love.

130 George Job Elvey
FS 3

Crown him with many crowns,
 The Lamb upon his throne;
Hark! how the heav'nly anthem drowns
 All music but its own;
Awake, my soul, and sing
 Of him who died for thee,
And hail him as thy matchless King
 Through all eternity.

Crown him the Son of God
 Before the world began,
And ye, who tread where he hath trod,
 Crown him the Son of man;
Who ev'ry grief hath known
 That wrings the human breast,
And takes and bears them for his own,
 That all in him may rest.

Crown him the Lord of life,
 Who triumphed o'er the grave,
And rose victorious in the strife
 For those he came to save;
His glories now we sing
 Who died, and rose on high,
Who died, eternal life to bring,
 And lives that death may die.

Crown him of lords the Lord,
 Who over all doth reign,
Who once on earth, the incarnate Word,
 For ransomed sinners slain,
Now lives in realms of light,
 Where saints with angels sing
Their songs before him day and night,
 Their God, Redeemer, King.

Crown him the Lord of heav'n,
 Enthroned in worlds above;
Crown him the King, to whom is giv'n
 The wondrous name of Love.
Crown him with many crowns,
 As thrones before him fall,
Crown him, ye kings, with many crowns,
 For he is King of all.

131 Jewish Doxology (Para. Thomas Oliver)
FS 4

The God of Abraham praise,
 Who reigns enthroned above;
Ancient of everlasting days,
 And God of love;
To him uplift your voice,
 At whose supreme command
From earth we rise, and seek the joys
 At his right hand.

He by himself hath sworn:
 I on his oath depend;
I shall, on eagle wings up-borne,
 To heav'n ascend:

I shall behold his face,
  I shall his power adore,
And sing the wonders of his grace
  For ever more.

There dwells the Lord, our King,
  The Lord, our righteousness,
Triumphant o'er the world and sin,
  The Prince of peace;
On Sion's sacred height
  His kingdom he maintains,
And, glorious with his saints in light,
  For ever reigns.

The God who reigns on high
  The great archangels sing,
And 'Holy, Holy, Holy,' cry,
  'Almighty King!
Who was, and is, the same,
  And evermore shall be:
Eternal Father, great I AM,
  We worship thee.'

The whole triumphant host
  Give thanks to God on high:
'Hail, Father, Son, and Holy Ghost!'
  They ever cry;
Hail, Abraham's God and mine!
  I join the heav'nly lays;
All might and majesty are thine,
  And endless praise.

132 Roy Turner FS 5

Hallelujah! Gonna sing all about it.
  Hallelujah! Gonna shout all about it.
Hallelujah! Can't live without it,
  Praise God. (Praise God.)
Now I'm living in a new creation,
  Now I'm drinking at the well of salvation.
Now there is no condemnation,
  Praise God. (Praise God.)

133 Tim Cullen FS 6

Hallelujah, my father,
  For giving us your Son,
Sending him into the world
  To be given up for men,
Knowing we would bruise him
  And smite him from the earth.
Hallelujah, my father,
  In his death is my birth.
Hallelujah, my father,
  In his life is my life.

134 Diane Davis FS 7

Refrain
Praise my God with the tambourine;
Sing to the Lord with the cymbals.

I will sing a new song to my God.
'You are great, you are glorious,
Wonderfully strong.'

'May your whole creation serve you.
When you speak, things come into being;
No one can resist your voice.'

'Should the mountains topple to mingle
    with the waves,
Should rocks melt like wax before your face,
To those who fear you,
    you would still be merciful.'

135 Roy Turner FS 8

David danced before the Lord,
  he danced with all his might;
His heart was filled with holy joy,
  his spirit was so light.
Michal through the window looked,
  to criticise did start,
She didn't know that David
  had got a dancing heart.

Refrain
Oh, the Holy Ghost will set your feet
    a-dancing!
The Holy Ghost will fill you
    through and through.
The Holy Ghost will set your feet a-dancing,
And set your heart a-dancing too!

David danced before the Lord
    to magnify his name;
In God's almighty presence
    he felt no sense of shame;
The oil of gladness flowed that day,
    it quickened every part;
He hadn't only dancing feet,
    he had a dancing heart.

Out of Egypt long ago the Israelites were led;
By a mighty miracle they all were
    kept and fed;
Through the Red Sea they were brought,
    the waters stood apart,
And God gave sister Miriam a dance
    down in her heart.

CELEBRATION

There was a celebration –
  upon the Red Sea shore;
Timbrels rang, desert sands
  became a dancing floor;
The people sang and praised God there,
  he made the gloom depart,
And put a dance of love and joy
  a-deep down in their hearts.

The prodigal was far away –
  wandering out in sin,
But he came back to Father's house
  and Father took him in;
He put a robe upon his son –
  the merriment did start,
The prodigal got dancing shoes
  to match his dancing heart.

The father's house with music
  rang to welcome home the son;
Wine was flowing full and free,
  all misery was gone;
The elder brother looking on complained
  it wasn't fair;
He hadn't got a dancing heart
  like all the others there.

Now many saints are cold
  and bound by unbelief today,
They want the blessings of the Lord
  but worry what men say;
Oh, let the Lord have full control,
  from dead traditions part,
And he will set you free within,
  you'll have a dancing heart.

136 Traditional
FS 9

Now let us sing,
  Sing 'til the power of the Lord comes down.
Now let us sing,
  Sing 'til the power of the Lord comes down.
Lift up your hands,
  Lift up your hands.
Don't be afraid.
  Don't be afraid.
Now let us sing 'til the power of the Lord
  comes down.

Now let us (praise, pray, love . . .)

or

Lift up your (hearts, heads . . .)

137 Jacob Krieger (Adapted by Mikel Kennedy)
FS 10

Refrain
Sing praise to the Lord for ever and ever,
Call unto him for hope and salvation.
Sing praise, alleluia, sing praise, allelu,
Sing praise, alleluia, sing praise, allelu.

Oh, sing praise to our Father in heav'n.
Sing unto the Lord.

Oh, sing praise to the Son of God.
Call unto his name.

Oh, sing praise to the Spirit of God.
Sing to the Lord of life.

138 Nancy Carr Newman
FS 11

Refrain
Sing, sing alleluia,
  Sing glory Jesus Christ,
Sing, sing alleluia,
  Behold the Lamb of God.

He rules the heavens, master of the earth.
All men now join together to praise the Lord.

Who is the King of glory? What is his name?
Jesus of Nazareth is his name.

Come ye who seek the Lord,
  place your trust in him.
Jesus will set you free to follow him.

139 Donald Fishel
FS 12

Refrain
Sing to the Lord a new song,
  Sing to the Lord a new song,
Sing to the Lord, sing to the Lord a new song.

God made the world in seven days.
Adam sinned and then all men fell away.
Jesus came to redeem my soul.
  He died upon the cross
  And he made me whole!

God said to Moses, 'Go and set
  my people free.
I will be your guide, just always follow me.'
Moses led the people through
  the parted Red Sea,
  Then they sang, and they danced,
  And they had a jubilee!

FRESH SOUNDS

Jesus said to Peter, 'Come on, I'm calling you.
I know the way is hard, but I'll always see
   you through.'
Peter said, 'My Lord, I'm a sinful man.'
  Then he threw down his net, and
  To the Lord he ran!

Come on my brother, won't you turn
   to Jesus now.
He knows that you're a sinner
But he loves you anyhow.
    Jesus paid the price for your salvation,
    Just call upon his name
      and you're a new creation!

Though I wander through desolation,
I will find you there.
Though the waters o'erwhelm my soul,
Even so you are Lord.

Create in me a new heart.
I would see your face.
Take not your holy Spirit from me,
I would see your face.

You have led us out of bondage,
You have kept us well.
Even in the face of our complaint,
You have loved us still.

140   Richard Gullen   FS 13

Refrain
We will sing to the Lord our God,
  mighty and splendid is he!
We will sing to our Saviour and King,
  glorious in majesty.

Here is the Lord, he is among us;
  Let us worship him together.
Here is the Lord, he is among us;
  Let us praise him all together.

Here is the Lord, let us walk with him;
  He will lead and guide us through his land.
Here is the Lord, let us walk with him;
  We will walk in peace throughout his land.

141   Charles High   FS 14

This is the day of the Lord
  This is the day of the Lord.
This is the day of the Lord.
  Allelu, allelu.

Adapt verses to suit occasion, such as:

This is the (feast, birthday, service, song)
  of the Lord . . .

We are the people of the Lord . . .

These are the praises of the Lord . . .

142   Jodi Page   FS 15

Refrain
Turn me, O God, and I shall be turned.
Turn me, O God, and I shall be turned.

143   Kathleen Thomerson   FS 16

Refrain
Jesus, I love you.
  Jesus, I love you.
Jesus, I love you,
  Take my life.

Life is your gift, I give my heart.
Kneel and adore You,
And I know that

Now I have seen the love of God.
He has poured out the Spirit of truth.

Love reaches out both near and far,
And so we follow where you lead us.
Jesus, I follow, Jesus, I follow,
Jesus, I follow, all my life.

144   Anon.   FS 17

Jesus, Jesus,
  Let me tell you what I know.
You have given us your spirit,
  We love you so.

145   Kathleen Thomerson   FS 18

I sing to the shepherd of my soul all the day
As he leads me through this world.
To follow him, to truly follow in his way
Is to live a life of love.

Refrain
All I am I offer Jesus,
  Singing praises unto him.
Oh, my soul, gives thanks to Jesus
  For he is your shepherd-king.

I sing to the shepherd of my soul all the night
For the path is clear to him.
And when I sleep, he makes a shelter
   of his light;
When I wake he leads me on.

All my life, O shepherd of my soul, I will sing
With a heart that's full of joy.
To follow you is just to trust that you will bring
All your sheep into the fold.

146   Anon.   FS 19

Come into his presence singing
   'Alleluia, Alleluia, Alleluia.'

Other verses may be added:
Come into his presence singing
   'Jesus is Lord,' . . .

Come into his presence singing
   'Worthy the Lamb,' . . .

Come into his presence singing
   'Glory to God,' . . .

147   Samuel Crossman   FS 20

My song is love unknown,
   My Saviour's love to me,
Love to the loveless shown,
   That they might lovely be,
O who am I, that for my sake
   My Lord should take frail flesh and die?

He came from his blest throne
   Salvation to bestow;
But men made strange, and none
   the longed for Christ would know.
But O, my friend, my friend indeed,
   Who at my need his life did spend.

Sometimes they strew his way
   And his sweet praises sing;
Resounding all the day
   Hosannas to their King.
Then crucify is all their breath,
   And for his death they thirst and cry.

They rise and needs will have
   My dear Lord made away;
A murderer they save,
   The Prince of life they slay,
Yet cheerful he to suffering goes,
   That he his foes from thence might free.

In life, no house, no home
   My Lord on earth might have;
In death, no friendly tomb,
   But what a stranger gave.
What may I say? Heaven was his home;
   But mine the tomb wherein he lay.

Here might I stay and sing,
   No story so divine;
Never was love, dear King,
   Never was grief like thine.
This is my friend, in whose sweet praise
   I all my days could gladly spend.

148   Kathleen Thomerson   FS 21

I love the name of Jesus, king of my heart,
   he is everything to me.
I bless the name of Jesus, reign in my life,
   show the Father's love so free.
Spirit of love, spirit of power,
   shine through eternity.
I love the name of Jesus, light of the world,
   let me walk each day with thee.

I love the name of Jesus, risen above,
   and he loves and prays for me.
I bless the name of Jesus, ruling on high
   with a glorious majesty.
Spirit of love, spirit of power,
   shine through eternity.
I praise the name of Jesus, Lord of my life,
   for he died to set me free.

I love the name of Jesus, splendour of God,
   and his face I long to see.
I bless the name of Jesus, shepherd of men;
   by his side I now can be.
Spirit of love, spirit of power,
   shine through eternity.
I praise the name of Jesus, for he is love,
   and that love he gives to me.

149   Anon.   FS 22

Blessed be the name, blessed be the name,
Blessed be the name of the Lord.

Jesus is the name, Jesus is the name,
Jesus is the name of the Lord.

Worthy to be praised, worthy to be praised,
Worthy to be praised is the Lord.

150
Mimi Farra
FS 23

Sing to the Lord,
Sing to the Lord of Lords.
Glory, glory,
Glory, glory,
Glory to the Lord.

Sing, oh sing to the Son of God,
Sing, for he is worthy of
Glory, glory,
Glory, glory,
Glory to the Son.

Sing, oh sing to the Lamb of God,
Sing, for he is worthy of
Glory, glory,
Glory, glory,
Glory to the Lamb.

Sing, oh sing to the Word of God,
The Word made flesh in Jesus Christ.
Glory, glory,
Glory, glory,
Glory Jesus Christ.

151
Anon.
FS 24

Sweet Jesus, sweet Jesus,
Lily of the valley,
Bright as the morning star.
Sweet Jesus, sweet Jesus,
He's the God of every nation,
Bless his name.

How I love him, how I love him,
Lily of the valley,
Bright as the morning star.
How I love him, how I love him,
He's the God of every nation,
Bless his name.

Jesus loves you . . .

Sweet Jesus . . .

152
Paul Goodwin
FS 25

Sweet Jesus, sweet Jesus,
What a wonder you are,
You are brighter than the morning star;
You are fairer, much fairer
Than the lily that grows by the wayside,
Precious, more precious than gold.

You are the rose of Sharon,
The fairest of the fair,
You are all my heart could e'er desire.

Sweet Jesus, sweet Jesus,
What a wonder you are,
You are precious, more precious than gold.

153
Anon.
FS 26

God gives peace like a river, peace like a river,
God gives peace like a river in my soul.
God gives peace like a river, peace like a river,
God gives peace like a river in my soul.

God gives love . . .

God gives joy . . .

God gives faith . . .

God gives hope . . .

God gives praise . . .

154
John S. B. Monsell
FS 27

O worship the Lord in the beauty of holiness,
Bow down before him, his glory proclaim;
With gold of obedience,
    and incense of lowliness,
Kneel and adore him, the Lord is his name.

Low at his feet lay thy burden of carefulness,
High on his heart he will bear it for thee,
Comfort thy sorrows
    and answer thy prayerfulness,
Guiding thy steps as may best for thee be.

Fear not to enter his courts in the slenderness
Of the poor wealth thou would'st reckon
    as thine;
Truth in its beauty, and love in its tenderness,
These are the offerings to lay on his shrine.

These, though we bring them in trembling
    and fearfulness,
He will accept for the name that is dear;
Mornings of joy give
    for evenings of tearfulness,
Trust for our trembling,
    and hope for our fear.

O worship the Lord in the beauty of holiness,
   Bow down before him, his glory proclaim;
   With gold of obedience,
      and incense of lowliness,
   Kneel and adore him, the Lord is his name.

155   W. R. Featherston   FS 28

My Jesus, I love thee, I know thou art mine,
For thee all the follies of sin I resign.
My gracious Redeemer, my Saviour art thou:
If ever I loved thee, my Jesus, 'tis now.

I love thee because thou hast first loved me
And purchased my pardon on Calvary's tree.
I love thee for wearing the thorns on thy brow:
If ever I loved thee, my Jesus, 'tis now.

I'll love thee in life, I will love thee in death,
And praise thee as long
      as thou lendest me breath;
And say when the death dew
      lies cold on my brow:
If ever I loved thee, my Jesus, 'tis now.

In mansions of glory and endless delight,
I'll ever adore thee in heaven so bright;
I'll sing with the glittering crown on my brow:
If ever I loved thee, my Jesus, 'tis now.

156   H. H. Lemmel   FS 29

Turn your eyes upon Jesus,
   Look full in his wonderful face;
And the things of earth
      will grow strangely dim
   In the light of his glory and grace.

157   Tr. Edward Caswall   FS 30

Jesus, the very thought of thee
   With sweetness fills the breast;
But sweeter far thy face to see,
   And in thy presence rest.

No voice can sing, no heart can frame,
   Nor can the memory find,
A sweeter sound than Jesus' name,
   The Saviour of mankind.

O hope of every contrite heart,
   O joy of all the meek,
To those who fall, how kind thou art!
   How good to those who seek!

But what to those who find? Ah, this
   No tongue nor pen can show;
The love of Jesus, what it is,
   None but his loved ones know.

Jesus, our only joy be thou,
   As thou our prize will be;
In thee be all our glory now,
   And through eternity.

158   Frederick William Faber   FS 31

My God, how wonderful thou art,
   Thy majesty how bright!
How beautiful thy mercy seat,
   In depths of burning light!

How dread are thine eternal years,
   O everlasting Lord,
By prostrate spirits day and night
   Incessantly adored!

O how I fear thee, living God,
   With deepest tenderest fears,
And worship thee with trembling hope,
   And penitential tears.

Yet I may love thee, too, O Lord,
   Almighty as thou art,
For thou hast stooped to ask of me
   The love of my poor heart.

How wonderful, how beautiful,
   The sight of thee must be,
Thine endless wisdom, boundless power,
   And aweful purity.

159   Mimi Farra   FS 33

Refrain
I will arise so early in the morning,
Rise to sing my Saviour's praises;
Rise with joy in my heart to greet the Lord
Who gives me life, everlasting life.

Now no more can sorrow
   And death cause me to fear; for

I will sing to the God of creation;
   I will sing to the Lord of love.

160 Mimi Farra
FS 34

Come and bless, come and praise,
　Come and praise the living God.
Allelu, allelu, alleluia, Jesus Christ.

Refrain
Allelu, allelu, alleluia, Jesus Christ.
Allelu, allelu, alleluia, Jesus Christ.

Come and seek, come and find,
　Come and find the living God.
Allelu, allelu, alleluia, Jesus Christ.

Come and hear, come and know,
　Come and know the living God.
Allelu, allelu, alleluia, Jesus Christ.

Come and bless, come and praise,
　Come and praise the Word of God;
Word of God, Word made flesh,
　Alleluia, Jesus Christ.

Seasonal verses:

Come behold, come and see,
　Come and see the newborn babe.
Allelu, allelu, alleluia, Jesus Christ.

Angel choirs sing above,
　'Glory to the Son of God!'
Shepherd folk sing below,
　'Allelu, Emmanuel!'

161 M. McAllister
FS 35

I trust in thee, O Lord.
　I say, 'Thou art my God.'
My times are in thy hand,
　My times are in thy hand.
Blessed be the Lord,
　For he has wondrously shown
His steadfast love to me,
　His steadfast love to me.

162 Ruth Wieting
FS 36

Refrain
O magnify the Lord with me,
Let us praise his name together.

I will bless the Lord at all times.
His praise will always be in my mouth.

I cried unto the Lord,
And he has freed me from all my fears.

O trust the Lord, you Saints,
For those who trust him lack no good thing.

O come, you Sons of God
To be the body of Jesus Christ.

163 Author unknown
FS 37

There is a river whose streams make glad
　The city of God, the city of God;
The holy habitation of the most high,
　The city of God, the city of God.
God is in the midst of her,
　She shall not be moved;
The Lord of hosts is with her.

164 Author unknown
FS 38

Refrain
O give thanks unto the Lord, for he is good,
　for his mercy endureth for ever.

O give thanks unto the God of Gods,
　for his mercy endureth for ever.
O give thanks unto the Lord of Lords,
　for his mercy endureth for ever.
To him who alone doeth great wonders,
　for his mercy endureth for ever. *Refrain*

To him that by wisdom made the heav'ns,
　for his mercy . . .
To him that stretched the earth
　　above the water,
　for his mercy . . .
To him that made great lights,
　for his mercy . . . *Refrain*

To him that smote Egypt in their first-born,
　for his mercy . . .
And brought out Israel from among them,
　for his mercy . . .
With a strong hand and with a stretched out
　　arm,
　for his mercy . . . *Refrain*

To him which divided the Red Sea,
　for his mercy . . .
And made Israel to pass
　　through the midst of it,
　for his mercy . . .
But overthrew Pharaoh and all his host,
　for his mercy . . . *Refrain*

To him which led his people
  through the wilderness,
  for his mercy . . .
To him which smote great kings,
  for his mercy . . .
And gave them land for an heritage,
  for his mercy . . . *Refrain*

Who remembered us in our low estate,
  for his mercy . . .
And hath redeemed us from our enemies,
  for his mercy . . .
O give thanks unto the God of heaven,
  for his mercy . . . *Refrain*

Christmas antiphon
Alleluia, Alleluia,
  for his mercy . . .
Unto us is born a Son, Alleluia,
  for his mercy . . .
And he shall rule with equity,
  for his mercy . . . *Refrain*

165 Author unknown FS 39

Refrain
Lord, you have fulfilled your word;
Now let your servant depart in peace.

With my own eyes I have seen the salvation,
Which you have prepared
  in the sight of every people:

A light to reveal you to the nations,
And the glory of your people Israel.

166 Author unknown FS 40

My soul doth magnify the Lord,
And my spirit hath rejoiced in God my Saviour
For he that is mighty hath done great things,
And holy is his name.

My soul doth magnify the Lord,
My soul doth magnify the Lord,
And my spirit hath rejoiced in God my Saviour
For he that is mighty hath done great things,
And holy is his name.

167 Traditional FS 41

Jesus, Lamb of God,
  Have mercy on us.
Jesus, bearer of our sins,
  Have mercy on us.

Jesus, redeemer of the world,
  Give us your peace.
  Give us your peace.

168 Thomas Ken (Verse 2: Deanne Wheeler) FS 42

Praise God from whom all blessings flow,
  praise him all ye creatures here below.
Praise him above, ye heavenly host,
  praise him Father, Son and Holy Ghost.

Hallelujah! Got the victory
  over Satan and over sin.
Jesus Christ is alive today, and he
  leads and guides me all the way.

Amen, amen, amen, amen, amen,
  Amen, amen, amen, amen.
Amen, amen, amen, amen, amen,
  Amen, amen, amen, amen.

169 Thomas Ken FS 43

Praise God from whom all blessings flow.
  Praise him, all creatures here below.
Praise him above, ye heavenly host.
  Praise Father, Son, and Holy Ghost.

170 Thomas Ken FS 44

Praise God from whom all blessings flow;
Praise him all creatures here below.
Praise him above ye heavenly hosts;
Praise Father, Son, and Holy Ghost.

171 Traditional FS 45

Our Father in heaven,
Hallowed be your name.
Your kingdom come, your will be done
On earth as in heaven.
Give us today our daily bread.
Forgive us our sins as we forgive
Those who sin against us.
Do not bring us to the time of trial
But deliver us from evil.
For the kingdom, the power and the glory
Are yours now and for ever. Amen.

172 Traditional
FS 46

Our Father who art in heaven,
　Hallowed be thy name.
Thy kingdom come, thy will be done,
　Hallowed be thy name.
On the earth as it is in heaven,
　Hallowed be thy name.
Give us this day our daily bread,
　Hallowed be thy name.
And forgive us all our trespasses,
　Hallowed be thy name.
As we forgive those who trespass against us,
　Hallowed be thy name.
And lead us not to the devil to be tempted,
　Hallowed be thy name.
But deliver us from all that is evil,
　Hallowed be thy name.
For thine is the Kingdom and the power
　and the glory,
　Hallowed be thy name.
For ever and ever and ever and ever,
　Hallowed be thy name.
Amen, amen, amen, amen,
　Hallowed be thy name.
Amen, amen, amen, amen,
　Hallowed be thy name.

173 Edith McNeill
FS 47

Refrain
The steadfast love of the Lord never ceases,
　His mercies never come to an end.
They are new every morning,
　　new every morning.
　Great is thy faithfulness, O Lord!
　Great is thy faithfulness.

The Lord is my portion, says my soul.
　Therefore I will hope in him.

The Lord is good to those who wait for him,
　To the soul that seeks him.
It is good that we should wait quietly
　For the salvation of the Lord.

The Lord will not cast off for ever,
　But will have compassion.
For he does not willingly afflict or grieve
　The sons of men.

So let us examine all our ways,
　And return to the Lord.
Let us lift up our hearts and hands
　To God in heav'n.

174 Jodi Page
FS 48

Refrain
Put on love, put on love,
And the peace of God that binds us all
　　together
Will keep our hearts in perfect harmony,
　If we put on love.

We are God's chosen race, his saints,
　And he loves us.
We should be clothed in peace,
　In kindness, and humility
As we . . .

God has forgiven us,
　Now we should forgive our brother.
We should show gentleness
　And bear with one another
As we . . .

Always be thankful and
　Let the message of Jesus
In all its richness
　Find a dwelling place in our hearts
As we . . .

175 Horatius Bonar
FS 49

I heard the voice of Jesus say,
'Come unto me and rest;
Lay down, thou weary one, lay down
Thy head upon my breast.'

I came to Jesus as I was,
Weary and worn and sad;
I found in him a resting-place,
And he has made me glad.

I heard the voice of Jesus say,
'Behold, I freely give
The living water; thirsty one,
Stoop down and drink, and live.'

I came to Jesus, and I drank
Of that life-giving stream;
My thirst was quenched, my soul revived,
And now I live in him.

I heard the voice of Jesus say,
'I am this dark world's light;
Look unto me, thy morn shall rise,
And all thy day be bright.'

I looked to Jesus, and I found
In him my star, my sun;
And in that light of life I'll walk
Till trav'ling days are done.

CELEBRATION

176 Refrain: L. E. Jones; Verses: Gary Miles
FS 50

My Jesus, he saves and heals me,
My body, spirit, soul.
My king and my shepherd leads me
And makes my body whole.

Refrain
Oh, there is power, power,
  wonder-working power
In the blood of the Lamb.
There is power, power,
  wonder-working power
In the precious blood of the Lamb.

He fills me to over-flowing,
  He comes as the dove,
My spirit and his united.
  Oh, wondrous, precious love.

Our Father, he made and loves us,
  He gave his only Son.
We'll see him one day in glory
  And join the Three in One.

177 Linda Rich
FS 51

They say that I'm a dreamer,
  Blind and cannot see
That life consists of living
  Only to earn money.
Well, you know who I am, Lord;
  You'll always care for me.
I only want to be like the
  Man of Galilee.

Refrain
I want to be like,
I want to hear like,
I want to see like
The man of Galilee.

They say that I'm an idealist,
  Blind and cannot see
That the principles I cling to
  Can't stand reality.
Well, I know who you are, Lord;
  You'll always care for me.
I only want to be like the
  Man of Galilee.

178 Jane and Betsy Clowe
FS 52

Refrain
Wind, wind, blow on me;
  Wind, wind, set me free;
Wind, wind, my Father sent
  The blessed Holy Spirit.

Jesus told us all about you,
  How we could not live without you,
With his blood the power bought to
  Help us live the life he taught.

When we're weary you console us;
  When we're lonely you enfold us;
When in danger you uphold us,
  Blessed Holy Spirit.

When unto the Church you came,
  It was not in your own but Jesus' name.
Jesus Christ is still the same,
  He sends the Holy Spirit.

Set us free to love our brothers;
  Set us free to live for others
That the world the Son might see
  And Jesus' name exalted be.

179 Brian Casebow
FS 53

Refrain
For the fruit of the Spirit is love, joy, peace,
  patience, kindness, goodness,
Faithfulness, gentleness, self-control;
  for such there is no law.

Have you seen my Lord on the cross so high?
Do you know his name? Do you hear his cry?
'Father, here's my love. Father, take my love,
  As the tree bears fruit for you.'

Have you seen his face and the look he gave
To the dying man he alone would save?
'Sinner, here's my love. Sinner, take my love,
  As the tree bears fruit for you.'

Can we answer him? Can the heart reply?
How to follow him as we live and die!
Jesus, here's our love. Jesus, take our love,
  As the tree bears fruit for you!

180 Jon Wilkes
FS 54

Refrain
Can men gather grapes from the thorns,
  Or figs from the thistled stem?
He that hath ears let him hear,
  By their fruits ye shall know them.

My friend came to man to show him
  how to love;
His blessing he gave to the meek.
Men took his love and they called it a lie,
  His answer was only this cry:
Refrain

In darkness they led him to priests and kings,
    They called him the Lord of the Flies.
Spat in his face and they crowned him
    with thorns:
    'Hail, the King of the Jews.'
Refrain

They nailed his hands and split his side,
    They cast the lots for his clothes.
The only comfort they had to give
    Was vinegar and gall.

Modified Refrain
Can men gather grapes from the thorns,
    Or figs from the thistled stem?
Father, forgive, – they know not what they do;
    By their fruits ye shall know them.

Brothers, oh judge the heart of mankind,
    The test is sure and true.
Eat of the fruit and savour the taste.
    What does it say to you?
Refrain

181   Nan Pagano / FS 55

Refrain
My God makes the flowers to bloom.
My God sends the rain.
    My God sets the rainbow in the sky,
    Hears each baby when he cries,
    And each mother as she sighs,
    Sent his only Son to die.
Oh, praise him,
My God is the only true and living God
And he has made me his child.

One day in spring while walking with the Lord,
    Listening to his word, I heard him say,
'This is my world and I have given it to you,
    Every colour, every hue,
Every breeze and drop of dew
    is from my hand.
Walk in the knowledge that the waters
    swirling round
And the rocks resound
    The praises of my name.'
My heart cried,

'When summer heat reveals
    the circumstance of life,
    The burden and the strife, call on my name.
Then autumn comes and all your world
    is turning brown,
The leaves are falling down
And the winter's cold is all around.
    It's from my hand.

Walk in the knowledge
    that the faith you have is seed
Sufficient to the need,
So claim my grace and live!'
My heart cried,

He spoke again and said,
    'You are a child of mine,
A branch upon the vine. Bring forth my
    fruit.'
My heart cried out, 'I see,
    it's all a gift from thee!
Let the seasons have their way, Lord,
Walk with me through night and day. It's
    from my hand.
I'll walk in knowledge
    that the spring will come again
And I will go rejoicing
In the fragrance of its bloom.'
My heart cried,

182   Marie Malone / FS 56

Israel is my vineyard and I, the Lord,
    Will tend the fruitful vines.
Every day I'll water them and day and night
    I'll watch to keep all enemies away. I'll . . .

Alleluia, alleluia, praise the Lord!
    Alleluia, praise his name!
Alleluia, alleluia, praise the Lord!
    Alleluia, praise his name.

183   Anon. / FS 57

Thou wilt keep him in perfect peace,
    Thou wilt keep him in perfect peace,
    Thou wilt keep him in perfect peace
Whose mind is stayed on thee.

Marvel not that I say unto you,
    Marvel not that I say unto you,
    Marvel not that I say unto you,
Ye must be born again.

Though your sins as scarlet be,
    Though your sins as scarlet be,
    Though your sins as scarlet be,
They shall be white as snow.

If the Son shall make you free,
    If the Son shall make you free,
    If the Son shall make you free,
Ye shall be free indeed.

They that wait upon the Lord,
They that wait upon the Lord,
They that wait upon the Lord,
They shall renew their strength.

Whom shall I send and who will go?
Whom shall I send and who will go?
Whom shall I send and who will go?
Here I am, Lord, send me.

184 Diane Davis
FS 58

Refrain
The Lord is a great and mighty king,
Just and gentle with every thing.
So with happiness we sing,
And let his praises ring.

We are his voice, we his song;
Let us praise him all day long. Alleluia!

We are his body here on earth;
From above he gave us birth. Alleluia!

For our Lord we will stand,
Sent by him to every land. Alleluia!

The Lord our God is one,
Father, Spirit and the Son. Alleluia!

185 John Ylvisaker
FS 59

Refrain
This is the feast of vict'ry for our God,
For the Lamb who was slain
    has begun his reign:
Alleluia.

Worthy is Christ, the Lamb who was slain,
Whose blood set us free
    to be people of God.
Power, riches, wisdom and strength
And honour, blessing and glory are his.

Sing with all the people of God
And join in the hymn of all creation:
'Blessing, honour, glory and might
Be to God and the Lamb for ever. Amen.'

186 Jodi Page
FS 60

Refrain
Please break this bread, Lord,
Please break this bread,
Bread of your body risen in us.

Pour out your wine, Lord,
Pour out your wine.
Let it flow through us to a thirsty world.

We've come to eat your bread,
Make us one.
We've come to drink your wine,
Make us one.
We've come in memory of your death
To give you thanks.
We've come to celebrate your life
And give you praise.

Let us be broken, O Lord,
To feed your sheep.
Let us be poured out, O Lord,
That men may see
That you are Spirit and life
That satisfy,
That you are risen in us
To set men free.

Last Refrain
Please break this bread, Lord,
Please break this bread.
Pour out your wine, Lord,
Pour out your wine.

187 Traditional
FS 61

Let us break bread together, we are one.
Let us break bread together, we are one.
We are one as we stand
    with our face to the risen Son.
Oh, Lord, have mercy on us.

Let us drink wine together, we are one.
Let us drink wine together, we are one.
We are one as we stand
    with our face to the risen Son.
Oh, Lord, have mercy on us.

Let us praise God together, we are one.
Let us praise God together, we are one.
We are one as we stand
    with our face to the risen Son.
Oh, Lord, have mercy on us.

188 Author unknown
FS 62

Anyone who does the will of God,
Anyone who does the will of God,
Anyone who does the will of God
Is my brother, my sister and mother.

189
Philip Doddridge
FS 63

Triumphant Zion, lift thy head
From dust and darkness and the dead;
Though humbled long, awake at length,
And gird thee with thy Saviour's strength.

Put all thy beauteous garments on,
And let thine excellence be known:
Decked in the robes of righteousness,
The world thy glories shall confess.

No more shall foes unclean invade,
And fill thy hallowed walls with dread;
No more shall hell's insulting host
Their vict'ry and thy sorrows boast.

God from on high has heard thy prayer,
His hand thy ruins shall repair:
Nor will thy watchful monarch cease
To guard thee in eternal peace.

190
Brian Howard
FS 64

What could be better than to come to dine
  On this bread and on this wine,
The bread of life and the cup of suffering,
  The body and blood of Jesus, our King?
I believe he's opened our eyes to really see
There's nothing better than
  to come to dine in unity.

What could be better than to carry the cross
  That our Lord has given us?
Just like his only begotten Son,
  He's chosen us to carry one.
I believe he's opened our eyes to really see
There's nothing better than
  to carry the cross in unity.

What could be better than to live in love
  With God's holy chosen ones,
Living together in unity, and out of that life
  The world to feed?
I believe he's opened our eyes to really see
There's nothing better than
  to live together in unity.

What could be better than to follow the Lord?
  In this whole wide world,
    there's nothing I'm sure.
So follow him we shall surely do.
  Listen, he's speaking to me and you.
I believe he's opened our eyes to really see
There's nothing better than
  to follow the Lord in unity.

191
William Williams
FS 65

Guide me, O thou great Jehovah,
  Pilgrim through this barren land;
I am weak, but thou art mighty,
  Hold me with thy powerful hand:
Bread of heaven, Bread of heaven,
  Feed me now and evermore,
  Feed me now and evermore.

Open thou the crystal fountain
  Whence the healing stream doth flow;
Let the fiery cloudy pillar
  Lead me all my journey through:
Strong deliv'rer, strong deliv'rer,
  Be thou still my strength and shield,
  Be thou still my strength and shield.

When I tread the verge of Jordan
  Bid my anxious fears subside;
Death of death, and hell's destruction
  Land me safe on Canaan's side:
Songs of praises, songs of praises,
  I will ever give to thee,
  I will ever give to thee.

192
Harry Emerson Fosdick
FS 66

God of grace and God of glory,
  On thy people pour thy power;
Crown thine ancient Church's story;
  Bring her bud to glorious flower.
Grant us wisdom, grant us courage,
  For the facing of this hour.

Lo! the hosts of evil round us
  Scorn thy Christ, assail his ways!
From the fears that long have bound us
  Free our hearts to faith and praise:
Grant us wisdom, grant us courage,
  For the living of these days.

Cure thy children's warring madness,
  Bend our pride to thy control;
Shame our wanton, selfish gladness,
  Rich in things and poor in soul.
Grant us wisdom, grant us courage,
  Lest we miss thy kingdom's goal.

Set our feet on lofty places;
  Gird our lives that they may be
Armoured with all Christ-like graces
  In the fight to set men free.
Grant us wisdom, grant us courage,
  That we fail not man nor thee.
    Amen.

CELEBRATION

193 Tim Whipple
FS 67

Refrain
Your kingdom come, your will be done,
 Now that we have become your sons.
 Let the prayer of our hearts daily be:
  God, make us your family.

The eyes of the blind shall be opened;
The ears of the deaf shall hear.
The chains of the lame will be broken;
Streams will flow in deserts of fear.

The ransomed of the Lord shall return;
The islands will sing his songs at last.
The chaff from the wheat shall be burned;
His kingdom on earth, it shall come to pass.

The nations will see their shame;
The one true God will be adored.
They turn from their fortune and shame;
His holy mountain shall be restored.

Optional Refrain for Christmastide
Laude, lauda, laude, lauda,
 Gloria Emmanuel.
Laude, lauda, laude, lauda,
 Gloria Emmanuel.

194 Maggie Durran
FS 68

Refrain
For we are a chosen race,
 a royal priesthood, holy nation.
 Once no people, now God's people,
 proclaiming his marvellous light.

Sing the songs of faithful Zion,
 We are the stars and the grains of sand.
Through our faith we are made glorious;
 We are Sons of Abraham.

Dance the steps of joyful Zion,
 Cymbals, harps and tambourines.
Blow the trumpet, sound the glory
 In the presence of the Lord.

Taste the fruit of peaceful valleys,
 Sip the wine and eat the bread.
Know the shepherd who is guiding,
 The Lord, the Lamb of God.

We will serve through tribulation,
 We will follow to the cross.
Know the death and pain of suffering;
 God wipes the tears from our eyes.

195 Clint Taylor
FS 69

Refrain
Comfort ye, comfort ye, my people.
Thus saith the Lord.

Bear each other up in your times of trouble,
Strengthen yourselves in your times of peace.

Love one another as I have loved you,
Everything else will fall into place.

Bless the Lord for his great mercy,
Especially for his Son Jesus Christ.

By my Spirit you have great power
Which enables you to do my work.

196 Brian Howard
FS 70

Refrain
Wherever two or more
 are gathered in my name,
 There I am, there I am;
Wherever two or more
 are gathered in my name,
 There I am in the midst of them.

Behold what manner of love the Father gives
 That we should be called the sons of God.
And now little children, abide in the Lord;
 We shall all be like him.

If we walk in the light as he is in the light,
 We shall always live with him;
For the blood of Jesus Christ
 Sets us free from sin.

197 Anon.
FS 71

In the name of Jesus, in the name of Jesus
 We have the victory.
In the name of Jesus, in the name of Jesus
 Demons will have to flee.
Who can tell what God can do?
Who can tell of his love for you?
In the name of Jesus, Jesus,
 We have the victory.

198 John S. B. Monsell
FS 72

Fight the good fight with all thy might,
Christ is thy strength and Christ thy right;
Lay hold on life, and it shall be
Thy joy and crown eternally.

Run the straight race through
  God's good grace,
Lift up thine eyes and seek his face;
Life with its way before us lies,
Christ is the path and Christ the prize.

Cast care aside, lean on thy Guide,
His boundless mercy will provide;
Trust, and thy trusting soul shall prove
Christ is its life and Christ its love.

Faint not, nor fear, his arms are near;
He changeth not, and thou art dear;
Only believe, and thou shalt see
That Christ is all in all to thee.

199 Mary Ackroyd
FS 73

Jesus is a-drivin' out Satan
  From ev'rywhere under the sun.
Jesus is a-drivin' out Satan,
  You'd better get up, Satan, and run.

Refrain
Jesus is the victor,
  Jesus, God's son.
Jesus is the King,
  The battle is won.

Jesus is a mighty warrior,
  He teaches us how to fight.
'Take my shield and my helmet
    and my double-edged sword.'
Satan fades in the sight of the right.

He gives us his blood and body;
  In his strength we must rest.
We aren't the ones who fight the battle
  When Satan puts us to the test.

You win the battle for us,
  We claim the power you give.
We are your lovin' people,
  And by your word we will live.

200 Refrain: John Yates; Verses: Betty Pulkingham
FS 74

If there's a mountain that needs to be moved,
If there's an obstacle right in your way,
Listen intently and God will speak to you.
Trust and obey him, come what may.

Refrain
Faith is the victory.
Faith is the victory.
Oh glorious victory
That overcomes the world.

Sarah and Abraham trusted God truly,
God promised them he would
  give them a son.
Many years passed, they were
  getting no younger;
Nothing's impossible, Isaac did come.

Three years and a half in the days of Elijah
It did not rain, the famine was sore.
Elijah prayed and a cloud appeared yonder;
He thanked God and it started to pour!

In times of war Gideon looked after his safety,
Shrinking behind the wine press was he.
God sent his angel who spoke to him thusly:
'You valiant and mighty man,
  God is with thee.'

201 Isaac Watts
FS 75

When I survey the wondrous cross
  On which the prince of glory died,
My richest gain I count but loss,
  And pour contempt on all my pride.

Forbid it, Lord, that I should boast
  Save in the cross of Christ my God;
All the vain things that charm me most,
  I sacrifice them to his blood.

See from his head, his hands, his feet,
  Sorrow and love flow mingling down;
Did e'er such love and sorrow meet,
  Or thorns compose so rich a crown?

Were the whole realm of nature mine,
  That were an off'ring far too small;
Love so amazing, so divine,
  Demands my soul, my life, my all.

202 Joan Hettenhouser
FS 76

I am persuaded that neither death, nor life,
  Nor angels nor principalities,
Nor powers, nor things present,
  Nor anything to come,
Nor height, nor depth,
  Nor any other creature
  Shall be able to separate us
From the love of God,
  Which is in Christ Jesus our Lord.

CELEBRATION

203
Samuel Stennett
FS 77

On Jordan's stormy banks I stand
 And cast a wishful eye
To Canaan's fair and happy land
 Where my possessions lie.

Refrain
I am bound for the promised land,
 I am bound for the promised land.
O who will come and go with me
 I am bound for the promised land.

When shall I reach that happy place
 And be for ever blest?
When shall I see my Father's face,
 And in his bosom rest?

204
Traditional
FS 78

Well, come go with me to that land,
 Come go with me to that land,
Come go with me to that land
 Where I'm bound.
Come go with me to that land,
 Come go with me to that land,
To that land, to that land,
 Where I'm bound.

There's gonna be lovin' in that land,
 Gonna be lovin' in that land,
Gonna be lovin' in that land
 Where I'm bound.
Gonna be lovin' in that land,
 Gonna be lovin' in that land,
In that land, in that land,
 Where I'm bound.

And milk and honey in that land . . .

Gonna meet Jesus in that land . . .

Be singin' and dancin' in that land . . .

Don't you know heaven is that land . . .

205
Author unknown
FS 79

He is my everything,
 He is my all,
He is my everything,
 Both great and small.
He gave his life for me,
 Made everything new.
He is my everything,
 He'll satisfy you.

206
Michael Baughen
FS 80

There's no greater name than Jesus,
 Name of him who came to save us,
In that saving name of Jesus
 Every knee should bow.
Let everything that is 'neath the ground,
 Let everything in the world around,
Let everything that's high o'er the sky
 Bow at Jesus' name.
In our minds by faith professing,
 In our hearts by inward blessing,
On our tongues by words confessing,
 Jesus Christ is Lord!

207
Philipp Bliss
FS 81

I am so glad that our Father in heav'n
Tells of his love in the book he has given.
Wonderful things in the Bible I see;
This is the dearest, that Jesus loves me.

Refrain
I am so glad that Jesus loves me,
 Jesus loves me, Jesus loves me,
I am so glad that Jesus loves me,
 Jesus loves even me.

Though I forget him and wander away;
Still he doth love me wherever I stray.
Back to his dear loving arms do I flee,
When I remember that Jesus loves me.

O, if there's only one song I can sing,
When in his beauty I see the great King,
This shall my song in eternity be,
O, what a wonder that Jesus loves me.

208
Anon.
FS 82

[Someone], Jesus loves you.
[Someone], Jesus loves you.
And love, love, love comes a'trickl'in' down.

Seek and ye shall find, ask anywhere,
Give a knock and the door shall be opened
And love, love, love comes a'trickl'in' down.

209
Ann House
FS 83

Jesus, Jesus loves [name].
 Yes, he does, yes, he does.
Jesus, Jesus loves [name].
 Yes, he does, yes, he does.

Jesus, Jesus loves [name].
  Yes, he does, yes, he does.
And he wants [name]
  To love him too.

210 Verses: Maggie Durran
FS 84

I walk with you, my children,
  Through valleys filled with gloom;
In echoes of the starlight
  And shadows of the moon.
In the whispers of the night-wind
  Are gentle words for you
To touch you and assure you
  It's my world you're walkin' through.

Refrain
And all creation's straining
  on tiptoe just to see
The sons of God
  come into their own.

I made the mottled stickleback
  To hide in crystal streams,
The staring owl to scan the night,
  The candle's gentle beams;
I made the silly camel
  To roam the desert sand,
But you I made, my children,
  To walk and hold my hand.

If life were filled with bubbles,
  They'd glisten and they'd burst;
If life were filled with jewels
  They'd line a rich man's purse;
But life is filled with water
  That flows from depths of love,
It flows to fill your weariness
  With blessing from above.

My love for you, my children,
  Puts rainbows in your hand,
Born of clouded sorrows
  In a sunburst morning land;
They arch above the smiling eyes
  Where tears can still be seen,
And adorn with gentle trembling touch
  The bride who is my own.

211 Lesbia Scott
FS 85

I sing a song of the saints of God,
Patient and brave and true,
Who toiled and fought and lived and died
For the Lord they loved and knew.

And one was a doctor, and one was a queen,
And one was a shepherdess on the green:
They were all of them saints of God
  and I mean
God helping to be one too.

They loved their Lord so dear, so dear,
  And his love made them strong;
And they followed the right, for Jesus' sake,
  The whole of their good lives long.
And one was a soldier, and one was a priest,
And one was slain by a fierce wild beast:
And there's not any reason, no, not the least,
  Why I shouldn't be one too.

They lived not only in ages past,
  There are hundreds of thousands still,
The world is bright with the joyous saints
  Who love to do Jesus' will.
You can meet them in schools, or in lanes,
  or at sea,
In church or in trains, or in shops or at tea,
For the saints of God are just folk like me,
  And I mean to be one too.

212 Betty Pulkingham
FS 86

Refrain
Ask, and it shall be given you.
  Seek, and ye shall find.
If you knock, knock, knock,
  The door will open unto you every time.

If a son shall ask his father
  For a piece of bread,
Will that father give his son
  A stone instead?

If a son shall ask his father
  For a little fish,
Will that father give him a serpent
  In his dish?

If a son shall ask his father for an egg
  Over light,
Will that father give him a scorpion
  That can bite?

If ye then, being evil,
  Know how to give good things,
How much more your loving
  Heavenly Father brings!
Your loving heavenly Father
  Gives the best gift of all,
He gives the Holy Spirit
  Unto them that call on him.

213
Max Dyer
FS 87

Pullin' the weeds, Lord, pullin' the weeds.
Livin' for your glory, pullin' the weeds.
(repeat)

Other suggested verses:

Sweepin' the floor Lord . . .

Goin' to school (church, bed, *etc!*), Lord . . .

Singin' this song, Lord . . .

214
Lisa Mazak (age 9)
FS 88

Refrain
One, two, three, Jesus loves me.
One, two, Jesus loves you.

Three, four, he loves you more
Than you've ever been loved before.

Five, six, seven, we're going to heav'n.
Eight, nine, it's truly divine.

Nine, ten, it's time to end;
But instead we'll sing it again.

Repeat, ending with 'There's no time to sing it again.'

215
Sherrell Prebble
FS 89

**Come with me to a land
where people are free,**
Where the lambs and the wolves roam
together through the country.
They say that a child can ride on a lion's back,
And not one man steals food
from his brother's shack.

Refrain
So put on your boots, let's get on the road.
There's just not that much time, you know.

It's a land for now, a land
where your spirit can live,
And eat the bread of life
that makes you whole.
When you're thirsty and you want a drink,
They have living water for your souls.

There you will find aching souls revived.
When the leader of that land passes by.
The lonely people find fellowship,
And there is plenty of healing for the sick.

216
Anon.
FS 90

Jesus took my burdens
and he rolled them in the sea,
Rolled them in the sea,
rolled them in the sea.
Jesus took my burdens
and he rolled them in the sea,
Never to remember any more.

Now I am happy, happy as can be,
Happy as can be, happy as can be.
Now I am happy, happy as can be,
Never to remember any more.

217
Anon.
FS 91

I must have Jesus in my whole life.
I must have Jesus in my life.
In my walking, in my talking,
In my sleeping, in my waking,
Must have Jesus in my life.

I have Christ Jesus in my whole life.
I have Christ Jesus in my life.
In my walking, in my talking,
In my sleeping, in my waking,
Have Christ Jesus in my life.

218
Diane Davis
FS 92

Refrain
I'm not alone for my Father is with me,
With me wherever I go.
Speaking words of faith, of courage
and of love,
He's with me, he loves me wherever I go.

Waking in the morning, getting ready
for school,
Walking down the road,
In class, at work, or at play,
He's with me, he loves me wherever I go.

And when I find myself in a mess,
I can trust in him,
Call on his name and watch him move,
He's with me, he loves me wherever I go.

All of my life everywhere that I go,
   I will walk with him,
Praising him and blessing his name,
   He's with me, he loves me wherever I go.

219   Author unknown — FS 93

Refrain
Put on the whole armour of God,
   Put on the whole armour of God,
Put on the whole armour of God,
   That you may stand against the devil
      and his wiles.

Take your stand with truth as your belt.
   Take your stand with truth as your belt.

Put on righteousness for your breastplate.
   Put on righteousness for your breastplate.

Shoe your feet with the gospel of peace.
   Shoe your feet with the gospel of peace.

As your helmet don salvation from God.
   As your helmet don salvation from God.

In your hand take the sword of the Spirit,
   Which is really the word of God.

Above all else take the shield of faith to
   Quench all the fiery darts of the wicked.

220   Author unknown — FS 94

Clean hands or dirty hands,
   Brown eyes or blue,
Pale cheeks or rosy cheeks,
   Jesus loves you.
Come to him while you may,
   Be his little lambs today.
Clean hands or dirty hands,
   Jesus loves you.

221   Robert Reynolds — FS 95

Bless you, Jesus, bless you.
Bless you, Jesus, bless you.
Bless you, Jesus, bless you.
All the people now, bless you.

Love you, Jesus . . .

Trust you, Jesus . . .

Serve you, Jesus . . .

Praise you, Jesus . . .

Last verse:
Amen, Jesus, amen.
Amen, Jesus, amen.
Amen, Jesus, amen.
All the people now *say*, 'Amen.'
                              (spoken)

222   Author unknown (Verse 2: Wendy Rhodes) — FS 96

He's my rock, my sword, my shield,
   He's the wheel in the middle of the wheel;
He's the lily of the valley
   The bright and morning star.
Makes no difference what you say,
   I'm going on my knees and pray,
I'm gonna see my Lord in glory
   One of these days.

Refrain
I'm gonna see my Lord in glory
   one of these days.
He's the rock of my soul and I'm gonna
   sing his praise.
   (Hallelujah.)
He's my rock, my sword, my shield,
He's the wheel in the middle of the wheel.
I'm gonna see my Lord in glory
   one of these days.

He's my peace, my joy, my love,
   My name's written in his book above,
He's the Captain of my company
   In the battle of the Lord.
Makes no difference what the devil may do,
I've got victory, how about you?
I'm gonna see my Lord in glory
   one of these days.

223   Traditionally ascribed to St. Francis of Assisi — FS 97

Make me a channel of your peace.
Where there is hatred let me bring your love;
Where there is injury, your pardon, Lord;
And where there's doubt, true faith in you.

Refrain
Oh, master, grant that I may never seek
So much to be consoled as to console;
To be understood as to understand;
To be loved, as to love with all my soul.

Make me a channel of your peace.
Where there's despair in life
   let me bring hope;
Where there is darkness, only light;
And where there's sadness ever joy.

Make me a channel of your peace.
It is in pardoning that we are pardoned,
In giving to all men that we receive;
And in dying that we're born to eternal life.

224   Donald Fishel   FS 98

Refrain
The light of Christ
  Has come into the world,
The light of Christ
  Has come into the world.

All men must be born again
  To see the Kingdom of God;
The water and the Spirit bring
  New life in God's love.

God gave up his only Son
  Out of love for the world,
So that all men who believe in him
  Will live for ever.

The light of God has come to us
  So that we might have salvation;
From the darkness of our sins we walk
  Into glory with Christ Jesus.

225   Diane Davis   FS 99

Refrain
It makes no difference who you are.
It makes no difference where you're going to,
When Jesus calls to you,
Drop everything and go, drop everything
   and go.

Peter was a fisherman,
He was fishing in his boat.
When Jesus called to him,
He dropped everything and he went,
He dropped everything and he went.

Laz'rus was dead and bound,
Dead and bound in his grave.
When Jesus called to him,
He dropped all his bonds and he went,
He dropped all his bonds and he went.

Jesus is the Son of God,
His Father called unto him,
Said, 'My people need to be redeemed.'
He took up his cross and he went
To die for you and me.

226   Sy Miller and Jill Jackson   FS 100

Let there be peace on earth
  And let it begin with me;
Let there be peace on earth,
  The peace that was meant to be,
With God as our Father,
  Brothers all are we,
Let me walk with my brother
  In perfect harmony.

Let peace begin with me,
  Let this be the moment now.
With ev'ry step I take,
  Let this be my solemn vow:
To God as our Father,
  Brothers all are we;
Let me walk with you my brother
  In perfect harmony.

Take each moment and
  Live each moment in peace eternally.
Let there be peace on earth
  And let it begin with me.

227   Carol Owens   FS 101

God forgave my sin in Jesus' name.
I've been born again in Jesus' name.
And in Jesus' name I come to you
To share his love as he told me to.

Refrain
He said,
Freely, freely, you have received,
  Freely, freely give.
Go in my name and because you believe
  Others will know that I live.

All power is given in Jesus' name.
In earth and heaven in Jesus' name.
And in Jesus' name I come to you
To share his power as he told me to.

228
Carey Landry
FS 102

Refrain
The spirit is a-movin' all over,
All over this land.

People are gatherin', the Church is born,
The Spirit is a blowin' on a world reborn.

Doors are opening as the Spirit comes,
His fire is burning in his people now.

Filled with the Spirit we are sent to serve,
We are called out as brothers,
We are called to work.

The world born once is born again,
We re-create it in love and joy.

Old men are dreaming dreams,
And young men see the light.

Old walls are falling down,
And men are speaking with each other.

The spirit fills us with his power
To be his witnesses to all we meet.

The Spirit urges us to travel light
To be men of courage who spread his fire.

God has poured out his Spirit
On all – on all of mankind.

229
East African folk song
FS 103

Refrain
Moto imeaka leo,
Moto nikazi ya Yesu,
Moto imeaka leo,
Tu imbe Hallelujah,
Moto imeaka,
Tu imbe Hallelujah,
Moto imeaka.

God's fire is burning in my soul,
God's fire is making me whole,
God's fire is sweeping o'er the earth.
Praise God, I've got God's fire
And it's burning in my soul,
Praise God, I've got God's fire
And it's burning in my soul.

God's power is burning . . .

God's Spirit is burning . . .

230
Author unknown
FS 104

When Jesus met with his disciples,
  When they'd all come together,
They asked him when he would restore
  The kingdom of Israel.

He told them that the time
  Was not for them to know,
The times and the seasons were his Father's,
  Only he would know.

But ye shall have power when the Spirit
  comes on you.
Ye shall be my witnesses to the ends
  of the earth;
To all Jerusalem, through all Judea,
  And in Samaria, to the ends of the earth.

231
Jodi Page
FS 105

Refrain
Come to the waters and I will give you rest.
Come to the waters and you will be refreshed.

Jesus said, 'Come unto me
  all ye weary, heavy laden.'

Jesus said of the waters that he gave,
  'He who drinks shall never thirst again.'

Jesus said, 'He who believes in me,
  out of him shall flow living waters.'

'So with joy ye shall draw water
  out of wells of salvation.'

232
Charles Wesley
FS 106

Jesus! the name high over all,
  In hell or earth, or sky;
Angels and men before it fall,
  And devils fear and fly,
  And devils fear and fly.

Jesus! the name to sinners dear.
  The name to sinners giv'n;
It scatters all their guilty fear,
  It turns their hell to heav'n,
  It turns their hell to heav'n.

Jesus! the pris'ners' fetters breaks,
　And bruises Satan's head;
Pow'r into strengthless souls it speaks,
　And life into the dead,
　And life into the dead.

O that the world might taste and see
　The riches of his grace;
The arms of love that compass me
　Would all mankind embrace,
　Would all mankind embrace.

His only righteousness I show,
　His saving grace proclaim;
'Tis all my business here below
　To cry: 'Behold the Lamb!'
　To cry: 'Behold the Lamb!'

Happy, if with my latest breath
　I might but gasp his name;
Preach him to all, and cry in death;
　'Behold, behold the lamb!'
　'Behold, behold the lamb!'

233 Author unknown
FS **107**

The Spirit of the Lord is upon me,
Because he has anointed me
To preach good news to the poor.
He has sent me to proclaim release
　　to the captives
And recovering of sight to the blind,
To set at liberty those who are oppressed,
To proclaim the acceptable year of the Lord.

234 Anna Withey (age 10)
FS **108**

Refrain
Come follow me now, come follow me now,
Come follow me now, said Jesus.

He died on the cross and bore all our pain.
I walk in his love, and he sends the rain
To water the plants that he gives to us.
And I do know he loves us.

I share my body with the whole of the world;
If you drink of my blood,
You will live evermore.
So follow me now, go tell the good news
That Christ is living in us.

CRY HOSANNA

235 Owen Barker
CH 1

How beautiful the morning and the day;
My heart abounds with music,
My lips can only say:
How beautiful the morning and the day.

How glorious the morning and the day;
My heart is still and listens,
My soul begins to pray
To him who is the glory of the day.

How bountiful the blessings that he brings
Of peace and joy and rapture
That make my spirit sing:
How bountiful the blessings that he brings.

How merciful the workings of his grace,
Arousing faith and action
My soul would never face
Without his matchless mercy and his grace.

How barren was my life before he came,
Supplying love and healing;
I live now to acclaim
The majesty and wonder of his name.

236 Lucy Morris
CH 2

Refrain
We want to bless you;
We want to praise you,
Jesus, our Lord.
(repeat)

In our weakness you are strong;
O Holy Spirit, lead us along.

O Prince of Peace, we call on you;
We worship you, praise you, love you, too.

The freedom you give is our delight;
We give ourselves to live in your light.

237 Anon.
CH 3

Praise ye the Lord always. *(repeat)*
Praise ye the Lord down in your heart;
Praise ye the Lord down in your heart always.

Jesus is Lord always. *(repeat)*
Jesus is Lord down in my heart;
Jesus is Lord down in my heart always.

I praise the Lord always. *(repeat)*
I praise the Lord down in my heart;
I praise the Lord down in my heart always.

238 Author unknown
CH 4

Refrain
Alabaré, alabaré,
  Alabaré a mi Señor.
(repeat)

John saw the number of all those redeemed,
And all were singing praises to the Lord.
Thousands were praying,
  ten thousands rejoicing,
And all were singing praises to the Lord.
Refrain

There is no God as great as you, O Lord,
  There is none, there is none.
(repeat)
There is no God who does
  the mighty wonders
That the Lord our God has done.
(repeat)
Neither with an army, nor with their weapons,
  But by the Holy Spirit's power.
(repeat)
And even mountains shall be moved, *(3 times)*
  By the Holy Spirit's power.
Refrain

*The following section may be sung several
times, using the names of different countries
(cities, etc.)*
And Puerto Rico shall be saved, *(3 times)*
  By the Holy Spirit's power.
Refrain

(238) Author unknown
CH (4)

Refrain
Alabaré, alabaré,
  Alabaré a mi Señor.
(repeat)

CELEBRATION

Juan vió el número de los redimidos,
  Y todos alababan al Señor.
Unos oraban, otros cantaban,
  Y todos alababan al Señor.
Refrain

No hay Dios tan grande como tu,
  No lo hay, no lo hay.
(repeat)
No hay Dios puede⌣hacer las cosas
  Como las que haces tu.
(repeat)
No es con espadas, ni con ejércitos,
  Más con su Santo⌣Espíritu.
(repeat)
Y esos montes se moverán, *(3 times)*
  Más con su Santo⌣Espíritu.
Refrain

The following section may be sung several times, using the names of different countries (cities, etc.)
Y Puerto Rico se salvará, *(3 times)*
  Más con su Santo⌣Espíritu.
Refrain

239 Wiley Beveridge and Bill Shehee
CH **5**

Part 1
O clap your hands, all you people;
  Shout unto God with a voice of triumph,
For God has gone up, gone up with a shout,
  The Lord with the sound of the trumpet.
(repeat)

Sing praise, sing praise to God,
  Sing praise unto our King.
Sing praise, sing praise to God,
  For God is the King of all the earth. *(repeat)*

Part 2
Hallelujah, glory be to God on high!
Hallelujah, glory be to God on high,
  Glory be to God on high!
(repeat)

Coda
Part 1
Hallelujah, hallelujah!
Hallelujah, hallelujah,
  Hallelujah!

Part 2
Hallelujah, glory be to God on high!
Hallelujah, glory be to God on high,
  Glory be to God on high!

240 vs. 1: Unknown; vs. 2: Rebekah Herold;
vs. 3: Jeff Cothran
CH **6**

Good morning, Jesus, good morning, love;
  We know you came from heaven above.
Your Holy Spirit moves like a dove.
  Good morning, Jesus, good morning, love.

Good morning, Jesus, good morning, light;
  You drive the darkness away like the night.
I couldn't see but now I walk with your sight.
  Good morning, Jesus, good morning, light.

Good morning, Jesus, dear Lord and King;
  We want to please you in everything,
And so with joy we lift our hearts up and sing,
  Good morning, Jesus, dear Lord and King.

241 Frank Hernandez
CH **7**

Hallelujah! Hallelujah!
He is Lord, he is Lord.
Hallelujah, Jesus is Lord!
(repeat)
Hallelujah, Jesus is Lord!

Hallelujah! Hallelujah!
He is King, he is King.
Hallelujah, Jesus is King!
(repeat)
Hallelujah, Jesus is King!

242 Gail Cole
CH **8**

The Lord is present in his sanctuary,
  Let us praise the Lord!
The Lord is present in his people
    gathered here,
  Let us praise the Lord!
    Praise him, praise him!
    Let us praise the Lord!
    Praise him, praise him!
    Let us praise Jesus!

The Lord is present in his sanctuary,
  Let us sing to the Lord!
The Lord is present in his people
    gathered here,
  Let us sing to the Lord!
    Sing to him, sing to him!
    Let us sing to the Lord!
    Sing to him, sing to him!
    Let us sing to Jesus!

The Lord is present in his sanctuary,
  Let us delight in the Lord!
The Lord is present in his people
    gathered here,
  Let us delight in the Lord!
    Delight in him, delight in him!
    Let us delight in the Lord!
    Delight in him, delight in him!
    Let us delight in Jesus!

The Lord is present in his sanctuary,
  Let us love the Lord!
The Lord is present in his people
    gathered here,
  Let us love the Lord!
    Love him, love him!
    Let us love the Lord!
    Love him, love him!
    Let us love Jesus!

243 Stephen Ball and Jon Wilkes
CH 9

Sing to our Father, Creator and King,
  Who sent his Son, Jesus, to suffer
    and bring us
  Into his family. Oh, magnify him!
    Sing, sing, sing, sing,
    Sing to the Lord of love!

Refrain
Alleluia, alleluia! *(repeat)*

Sing to our brother, who of himself poured out
  Life to his people to see them restored.
Sing to our healer and sing to our Lord!
  Sing, sing, sing, sing,
  Sing to the Lord of life!

Sing to the Spirit, let us all hear
  And know that he frees us from sin
    and from fear
To love one another, to serve and to care.
  Sing, sing, sing, sing,
  Sing to the Lord of peace!

244 Author unknown
CH 10

Jubilate Deo, jubilate Deo, alleluia!

CRY HOSANNA

245 Charles Christmas
CH 11

Refrain
Glory hallelujah! *(repeat)*

Give thanks to our God and let him be praised
With sanctified hearts and hands
    that are raised.
Come join a song of praise to our God.

His words ever true, the Son of his love.
Sing, men of earth, to the heavens above.
Honour and glory belong to our God.

Worthy the Lamb who was slain for our sins.
He laid down his life, he rose up again.
To us he gives unending life.

Holy, holy the Lord God almighty
Who was, who is, and who is to come.
In glory come, Lord Jesus, come.

246 Anon.
CH 12

Gloria, Gloria, Gloria in excelsis Deo.
(3 times)

247 Isaac Watts
CH 13

Before the Lord Jehovah's throne,
  Ye nations, bow with sacred joy;
  Know that the Lord is God alone;
  He can create, and he destroy.

His sov'reign power without our aid
  Made us of clay, and formed us men;
And when like wand'ring sheep we strayed,
  He brought us to his fold again.

We are his people, we his care,
  Our souls, and all our mortal frame:
What lasting honours shall we rear,
  Almighty Maker, to thy name?

We'll crowd thy gates with thankful songs,
  High as the heav'n our voices raise;
And earth, with her ten thousand tongues,
  Shall fill thy courts with sounding praise.

Wide as the world is thy command,
  Vast as eternity thy love;
Firm as a rock thy truth must stand,
  When rolling years shall cease to move.
  Amen.

CELEBRATION

248
Brian Howard
CH 14

This, this is the day that the Lord has made.
(repeat)
This is the day that the Lord has made;
   Let us rejoice and be glad in it.
This is the day that the Lord has made;
   Let us rejoice and be glad in it!

Great, great is the name of the Lord our God.
(repeat)
Great is the name of the Lord our God;
   We will rejoice and be glad in him.
Great is the name of the Lord our God;
   We will rejoice and be glad in him!

Sing, sing out his praise throughout the land.
(repeat)
Sing out his praise throughout the land;
   Now is the kingdom of God at hand.
Sing out his praise throughout the land;
   The kingdom of God is at hand!

Trust, trust in the Lord, all you who sing.
(repeat)
Trust in the Lord, all you who sing,
   Giving thanks and praise in everything.
Trust in the Lord, all you who sing,
   Giving thanks and praise in everything!
Repeat first verse.

249
Cecilie Hobson
CH 15

There's a river of praise within my heart
   Which is flowing full and free,
For Jesus Christ came down from heav'n;
   He died to set me free.
He took away my fear and shame
   By the pow'r of his great love;
So now I want to praise his name,
   All other names above.

He gives me joy as a garment of praise
   And by his Spirit, peace.
His ways are ways of gentleness;
   All anxious cares can cease.
For the love of the Lord is a deep, deep love
   Which flows eternally.
It reaches the depths of the human heart;
   It reaches you and me.

Then come to us, Lord, and touch our lives
   With your healing and your peace.
Fill us anew with your tender love,
   Deep springs of joy release.

So shall we bless and worship you
   And all our praises bring
To magnify your holy name,
   Jesus, our Lord and King.

250
Kevin O'Neill
CH 16

Refrain
Clap your hands, clap your hands,
   Sing unto the Lord, give all you can!
Clap your hands, clap your hands,
   Sing unto the Lord, all ye lands!
O let us sing, sing, sing to the Lord;
   For in his life our lives have been restored.

Open your eyes, it's a brand new day;
   Look and see the stone's been rolled away!
Open your heart and prepare the way:
   Don't be afraid to stand and say:

See his hands and see his side;
   Risen from the dead is he who died.
Run and tell the world that he's heard our cry
   And offers his life to satisfy.

If the Son has set us free,
   Then we shall be free indeed.
See how pleasant it can be
   For us to live in unity!

251
Mike Beck
CH 17

Fill your heart with love;
   God is love.
Fill your life with song;
   God be praised.

Glory in the highest!
Hosanna, hosanna to the Lord!

252
H. F. Lyte
CH 18

Praise, my soul, the King of heaven,
   To his feet thy tribute bring;
Ransomed, healed, restored, forgiven,
   Who like me his praise should sing?
     Alleluia! Alleluia!
   Praise the everlasting King.

Praise him for his grace and favour
  To our fathers in distress;
Praise him still the same as ever,
  Slow to chide, and swift to bless:
    Alleluia! Alleluia!
    Glorious in his faithfulness.

Father-like, he tends and spares us,
  Well our feeble frame he knows;
In his hands he gently bears us,
  Rescues us from all our foes:
    Alleluia! Alleluia!
    Widely as his mercy flows.

Angels, help us to adore him;
  Ye behold him face to face;
Sun and moon, bow down before him,
  Dwellers all in time and space:
    Alleluia! Alleluia!
    Praise with us the God of grace.

253 Timothy Dudley-Smith
CH 19

Tell out, my soul, the greatness of the Lord!
  Unnumbered blessings,
    give my spirit voice;
Tender to me the promise of his word;
  In God my Saviour shall my heart rejoice.

Tell out, my soul, the greatness of his name!
  Make known his might, the deeds his arm
    has done;
His mercy sure, from age to age the same;
  His holy name – the Lord, the mighty one.

Tell out, my soul, the greatness of his might!
  Pow'rs and dominions lay their glory by.
Proud hearts and stubborn wills
    are put to flight,
  The hungry fed, the humble lifted high.

Tell out, my soul, the glories of his word!
  Firm is his promise, and his mercy sure.
Tell out, my soul, the greatness of the Lord
  To children's children and for evermore!

254 Brent Chambers
CH 20

In the presence of your people
  I will praise your name,
  For alone you are holy,
    enthroned on the praises of Israel.

Let us celebrate your goodness
  and your steadfast love.
May your name be exalted
  here on earth and in heav'n above.

Lai lai lai lai lai lai lai lai
  lai lai . . .

255 Jan Harrington
CH 21

I will rejoice in the Lord alway. *(repeat)*
  Though the fig trees are barren
    And the cattle all die,
  And the crops have failed
    And the fields empty lie;
  And though he slay me,
    Even though he slay me,
  Yet I'll rejoice in the Lord alway.

Other verses may be added:
I will trust in the Lord alway. *(repeat)*
  Though the fig trees are barren
    And the cattle all die,
  And the crops have failed
    And the fields empty lie;
  And though he slay me,
    Even though he slay me,
  Yet I will trust in the Lord alway.

I will sing to the Lord alway . . .

I will delight in the Lord alway . . .

I will hope in the Lord alway . . .

256 Louise Jolly
CH 22

Blessing and honour and glory and pow'r,
Be yours for ever and ever. Amen.

257 Charles Wesley
CH 23

O for a thousand tongues to sing
  My great Redeemer's praise,
  The glories of my God and King,
    The triumphs of his grace!

Jesus, the name that charms our fears,
  That bids our sorrows cease;
'Tis music in the sinner's ears,
  'Tis life and health and peace.

He breaks the pow'r of cancelled sin,
  He sets the prisoner free;
His blood can make the foulest clean,
  His blood availed for me.

He speaks; and, list'ning to his voice,
  New life the dead receive,
The mournful broken hearts rejoice,
  The humble poor believe.

Hear him, ye deaf; his praise, ye dumb,
  Your loosened tongues employ;
Ye blind, behold your Saviour come;
  And leap, ye lame, for joy!

My gracious Master and my God,
  Assist me to proclaim
And spread through all the earth abroad
  The honours of thy name.

258 Dale Garratt — CH 24

Hallelujah, for the Lord our God,
    the Almighty, reigns!* (repeat)*
  Let us rejoice and be glad
  And give the glory unto him.
Hallelujah, for the Lord our God,
  the Almighty, reigns!

259 Rebecca MacVean — CH 25

Jesus, your blood has made me whole.
Jesus, your blood washed me white as snow.

Father, your love has set me free.
Father, your love lets me be me.

Spirit of God, you comfort me.
Spirit of God, you make my eyes see.

260 Robert Stoodley — CH 26

Jesus my Saviour,
  Oh, how I love you,
For you have filled me
  With your new life.

All your heav'nly glory
  You counted as nothing,
And bore the pain of death
  To make us free.

Therefore with all my heart
  I'll gladly sing your praise,
And do so all my days
  To bless your holy name.

For God has exalted you,
  Seated at the Father's side.
You shall be glorified,
  Jesus, our King!

261 Wiley Beveridge — CH 27

Jesus, Jesus, Jesus.

Spirit, sweet Spirit, fill my heart.

Father, oh, Father, take my heart.

262 Isaac Watts — CH 28

When I survey the wondrous cross
  Where the young Prince of Glory died,
My richest gain I count but loss,
  And pour contempt on all my pride.

Forbid it, Lord, that I should boast,
  Save in the cross of Christ, my God:
All the vain things that charm me most,
  I sacrifice them to his blood.

See, from his head, his hands, his feet,
  Sorrow and love flow mingled down!
Did e'er such love and sorrow meet,
  Or thorns compose so rich a crown?

Were the whole realm of nature mine,
  That were an off'ring far too small;
Love so amazing, so divine,
  Demands my soul, my life, my all.

263 Richard Gillard — CH 29

Worthy the Lamb that was slain for us.
Worthy, worthy the Lamb.

Blessed the Lamb . . .

Holy the Lamb . . .

Mighty the Lamb . . .

Jesus, the Lamb . . .

CRY HOSANNA

264   Jan Harrington   CH 30

All the riches of his grace,
  All the fullness of his blessings,
All the sweetness of his love
  He gives to you, he gives to me.
(repeat)

Oh, the blood of Jesus, *(3 times)*
It washes white as snow.

Oh, the word of Jesus, *(3 times)*
It cleanses white as snow.

Oh, the love of Jesus, *(3 times)*
It makes his body whole.

265   Anon.   CH 31

Jesus, you're a wonder; *(3 times)*
You're a wonder to my soul.

Refrain
  Glory, hallelujah! *(3 times)*
  You're a wonder to my soul.

Other verses may be added:
Jesus, you're the healer; *(3 times)*
You're the healer of my soul.

Refrain
  Glory, hallelujah! *(3 times)*
  You're the healer of my soul.

Jesus, you're the sunshine . . . lover . . .
    Saviour, *etc.*

266   Edith McNeill   CH 32

Refrain
Bless the holy name of Jesus, Jesus,
  Praise his glorious name!
Lord of life and our redeemer, saviour,
  Glory to his name!

Jesus, our shepherd, our light and salvation,
  Every day the same.
Bless the holy name of Jesus, Jesus,
  Glory to his name!

Jesus, we worship you, we praise
    and adore you,
  We exalt your name.
Bless the holy name of Jesus, Jesus,
  Glory to his name!

267   Philip Moore   CH 33

Jesus is Lord, Jesus is Lord, alleluia. *(repeat)*
Alleluia, alleluia. *(repeat)*

268   Patricia Cain   CH 34

Jesus, name above all names,
  Beautiful Saviour, glorious Lord,
Emmanuel – God is with us,
  Blessed Redeemer, living Word.

269   Audrey Mieir   CH 35

His name is wonderful, his name is wonderful,
  His name is wonderful, Jesus, my Lord.
He is the mighty King, master of everything,
  His name is wonderful, Jesus, my Lord.
He's the great shepherd, the rock of all ages,
  Almighty God is he!
Bow down before him, love and adore him;
  His name is wonderful, Jesus, my Lord.

270   Martha Butler   CH 36

I looked up and I saw my Lord a-coming,
I looked up and I saw my Lord a-coming
    down the road.

Refrain
Alleluia, he is coming,
Alleluia, he is here.
(repeat)

I looked up and I saw my Lord a-weeping,
I looked up and I saw my Lord a-weeping
    for my sins.

I looked up and I saw my Lord a-dying,
I looked up and I saw my Lord a-dying
    on the cross.

I looked up and I saw my Lord a-rising,
I looked up and I saw my Lord a-rising
    from the grave.

271   Tedd Smith   CH 37

There's a quiet understanding
  When we're gathered in the Spirit,
It's a promise that he gives us
  When we gather in his name.

CELEBRATION

There's a love we feel in Jesus,
   There's a manna that he feeds us,
It's a promise that he gives us
   When we gather in his name.

And we know when we're together,
   Sharing love and understanding,
That our brothers and our sisters
   Feel the oneness that he brings.

Thank you, thank you, thank you, Jesus,
   For the way you love and feed us,
For the many ways you lead us;
   Thank you, thank you, Lord.
   Thank you, thank you, Lord.

272 Jan Harrington
CH **38**

Jesus came and died on the tree,
   Rose again for you and me;
Now he lives so we can be free.
   Praise the name of Jesus.

273 Carey Landry
CH **39**

Refrain
O Lord, our God,
   We lift up our hearts to you.
O Lord, our God,
   Your people rejoice in you.

God of the living,
God of all people,
Father of life,
   We lift up our hearts to you.

Christ Jesus crucified,
Wounded for mankind,
You gave your life for us,
   We lift up our hearts to you.

Great Holy Spirit,
Bright fire of God,
Come, burn in our hearts, O Lord,
   We lift up our hearts to you.

Additional verses may be improvised, e.g.
River of mercy,
Oh, sea of peace,
Ocean of loveliness,
   We lift up our hearts to you.

274 Joseph Hart
CH **40**

Come, ye sinners, poor and needy,
   Weak and wounded, sick and sore;
Jesus ready stands to save you,
   Full of pity, love, and pow'r.

Refrain
I will arise and go to Jesus,
   He will embrace me in his arms;
In the arms of my dear Saviour,
   Oh, there are ten thousand charms.

Come, ye thirsty, come, and welcome,
   God's free bounty glorify;
True belief and true repentance,
   Every grace that brings you nigh.

Come, ye weary, heavy laden,
   Lost and ruined by the fall;
If you tarry till you're better,
   You will never come at all.

275 Edward Henry Bickersteth
CH **41**

Peace, perfect peace, in this dark world of sin?
The blood of Jesus whispers peace within.

Peace, perfect peace, by thronging duties
   pressed?
To do the will of Jesus, this is rest.

Peace, perfect peace, with sorrows
   surging round?
On Jesus' bosom naught but calm is found.

Peace, perfect peace, with loved ones
   far away?
In Jesus' keeping we are safe, and they.

Peace, perfect peace, our future all unknown?
Jesus we know, and he is on the throne.

Peace, perfect peace, death shadowing
   us and ours?
Jesus has vanquished death
   and all its powers.

It is enough: earth's struggles
   soon shall cease,
And Jesus call us to heav'n's perfect peace.

276 Author unknown
CH 42

The fear of the Lord is the beginning
of wisdom,
And the knowledge of the Holy
is understanding.

277 Mimi Farra
CH 43

Refrain
Trust in the Lord with all thine heart,
Lean not unto thine own understanding;
In all thy ways acknowledge him,
And he shall direct thy paths.

So shalt thou walk in thy way safely;
Thy foot, thy foot shall not stumble.
And when thou liest down,
Thy sleep, thy sleep shall be sweet.

Yea, if thou criest after knowledge,
And liftest up thy voice for understanding,
Thou shalt know the fear of the Lord,
And find the knowledge of God.

278 John McNeil
CH 44

Refrain
Sound on the trumpet, call to the people,
Sing your new song.
Our bridegroom's coming,
It won't be long.
Break out the banners, join in the dancing,
No time for gloom.
Prepare the banquet,
He's coming soon.

If you're one of God's people,
Rejoice in praise and song.
Come, lift up your hearts before him
And give your voices in praise and song.

Go out with tears and weeping
To bring the harvest home.
It's time for the joy of reaping;
In joy the sheaves now are coming home.

279 Richard Blanchard
CH 45

Like the woman at the well I was seeking
For things that could not satisfy.
And then I heard my Saviour speaking:
'Draw from my well that never shall run dry.'

Refrain
Fill my cup, Lord, I lift it up, Lord.
Come and quench this thirsting of my soul.
Bread of heaven, feed me till I want no more.
Fill my cup, fill it up and make me whole.

There are millions in this world
who are craving
The pleasure earthly things afford.
But none can match the wondrous treasure
That I find in Jesus Christ, my Lord.

So, my [brother/sister,] if the things
this world gave you
Leave hungers that won't pass away,
My blessed Lord will come and save you,
If you kneel to him and humbly pray.

280 Stuart Hamblen
CH 46

They that wait upon the Lord shall renew
their strength.
They shall mount up with wings as the eagle.
They shall run and not be weary,
They shall walk and not faint.
Teach me, Lord, teach me, Lord, to wait.

281 Diane Davis Andrew
CH 47

Refrain
Come, Lord Jesus, with healing hands
That bind us together in unity.
(repeat)

Take from us our words that sound
full of peace,
But are only subtle weapons
To separate us from each other.

Take from us our fear that keeps us bound,
Unable to reach out
And comfort one another.

Fill us with your Holy Spirit.
Create in us a new heart
That reaches out to hold each other.

282 Geoffrey Studdert-Kennedy
CH 48

Awake, awake to love and work!
The lark is in the sky,
The fields are wet with diamond dew,
The worlds awake to cry
Their blessings on the Lord of life,
As he goes meekly by.

CELEBRATION

Come, let thy voice be one with theirs,
  Shout with their shout of praise;
See how the giant sun soars up,
  Great lord of years and days!
So let the love of Jesus come
  And set thy soul ablaze.

To give, and give, and give again
  What God hath given thee;
To spend thyself nor count the cost;
  To serve right gloriously
The God who gave all worlds that are,
  And all that are to be.

283 Jodi Page Clark
CH 49

Refrain
Fear not, for I have redeemed you;
  I have called you by name.
I have called you by name;
  You are mine.

When you pass through the waters
  I will be with you;
  And through rivers, they will not
    overwhelm you.
When you walk through the fire
  you will not be burned;
  The flames shall not consume you.

Because you are precious and I love you,
  You whom I formed for my glory,
You whom I called by my name,
  I will gather together.

You are my witnesses; I have chosen you
  That you may know and believe me.
You are my servants for the world to see
  I am the Lord, I'm among you.

It's time now to lay aside the former things;
  A new day has dawned, do you see it?
I'm making a way in the wilderness,
  And rivers to flow in the desert.

The rivers that flow in the desert
  Give drink to my chosen people;
To quench their thirst and to strengthen them,
  That they might show forth my praise.

284 Anon.; Verses: Jan Harrington
CH 50

Refrain
Tell my people I love them,
  Tell my people I care.
When they feel far away from me,
  Tell my people I am there.

Tell my people I came and died
  To give them liberty,
And to abide in me
  Is to be really free.

Tell my people where'er they go
  My comfort they can know.
My peace and joy and love
  I freely will bestow.

285 Mimi Farra
CH 51

Pure light of the Son of God,
  Shine on my path that I may see
The way wherein you have called me to go.
  Shine on my path that I may follow you.

Pure mind of the Son of God,
  Come and think your thoughts in me.
One thought only would I know:
  Son of God, you love me so.

Pure love of the Son of God,
  Fill my heart that I may show
The love you have for all mankind,
  Love that is eternal life.

Spirit of the Son of God,
  Live in me that I may do
The will of God and be set free
  To live the life of Jesus Christ.

Jesus Christ, who sets us free,
  Calls to you and calls to me
To follow him to the Father's throne,
  There to dwell for eternity.

286 Sandy Hardyman
CH 52

Refrain
Lord, give us your Spirit,
  Your Spirit that is love.
Lord, fill us with your life,
  Freely given for the world.

Where children cry
  Let us wipe their tears away,
And where children fall
  Let us raise them to their feet.

Where there is pain
  Let us be your healing hands,
And where there is grief
  Let us comfort with your love.

Where people hate
  Let us dwell among them with love,
And where people fight
  Let us bind their deepest wounds.

287 Max Dyer
CH 53

Refrain
Allelu, 'lu-ia, 'lu-ia,
  Allelu, 'lu-ia, 'lu-ia.
Allelu, 'lu-ia, 'lu-ia,
  Allelu, 'lu-ia, 'lu-ia.

Feel a change a-comin', 'lu-ia, 'lu-ia,
  Feel a change a-comin', 'lu-ia, 'lu-ia,
Feel a change a-comin', 'lu-ia, 'lu-ia,
  I will sing to you.

Additional verses may be added, e.g.
Packed my bags today, 'lu-ia, 'lu-ia,
  Goin' far away, 'lu-ia, 'lu-ia,
Whether I go or stay, 'lu-ia, 'lu-ia,
  I will sing to you.

Pillar of cloud by day, 'lu-ia, 'lu-ia,
  Pillar of fire by night, 'lu-ia, 'lu-ia,
By the Spirit we are led, 'lu-ia, 'lu-ia,
  We will sing to you.

Last verse
Praise to the Father, 'lu-ia, 'lu-ia,
  Praise to the Son, 'lu-ia, 'lu-ia,
Praise to the Holy Spirit, 'lu-ia, 'lu-ia,
  Our Lord God, Three in One.

288 John Smith
CH 54

There's a new song in the land: *(3 times)*
  Jesus is Lord.
Jesus is Lord, he is Lord for evermore.
  Jesus is Lord.

There's a new song in the land: *(3 times)*
  Jesus is King.
Jesus is King, he is King for evermore.
  Jesus is King.

There's a new song in the land: *(3 times)*
  Jesus is Peace.
Jesus is Peace, he is Peace for evermore.
  Jesus is Peace.

There's a new song in the land: *(3 times)*
  Jesus is Love.
Jesus is Love, he is Love for evermore.
  Jesus is Love.

289 Sherrell Prebble and Howard Clark
CH 55

Refrain
Alleluia! Alleluia!
  Opening our hearts to him,
Singing alleluia! Alleluia!
  Jesus is our King!

Create in us, O God,
A humble heart that sets us free
To proclaim the wondrous majesty
  Of our Father in heaven.

We bear the name of Christ.
Justified, we meet with him.
His words and presence calm our fear,
  Revealing God, our Father, here.

Let kindred voices join,
Honouring the Lamb of God
Who teaches us by bread and wine
  The myst'ry of his body.

Pour out your Spirit on us,
Empowering us to live as one,
To carry your redeeming love
  To a world enslaved by sin.

290 William Alexander Percy
CH 56

They cast their nets in Galilee
  Just off the hills of brown;
Such happy, simple fisherfolk,
  Before the Lord came down.

Contented, peaceful fishermen,
  Before they ever knew
The peace of God that filled their hearts
  Brimful, and broke them too.

Young John who trimmed the flapping sail,
  Homeless, in Patmos died.
Peter, who hauled the teeming net,
  Head-down was crucified.

The peace of God, it is no peace,
  But strife closed in the sod.
Yet, brothers, pray for but one thing:
  The marv'lous peace of God.

291 Anon. (Tr. Susan Abbott)
CH 57

People of God,
People chosen, consecrated to our God,
Now sing the wonders he has done.

CELEBRATION

Refrain
We glorify our God on high,
Celebrate his gracious love
Alleluia, alleluia!

It is the Lord,
He who proclaims his word and
　bids us come to him,
Speaks to our souls and gives us life.

It is the Lord,
He who feeds his chosen ones
　on heav'nly food,
Pours out his life and makes us one.

　　　* * * *

Pueblo de Dios, pueblo elegido y consagrado
Para cantar las maravillas del Señor:

Refrain
¡Glorifiquemos a nuestro Dios,
Y celebremos su gran amor,
Aleluya, aleluya!

Es el Señor quien nos anuncia su palabra,
Es el Señor quien nos invita a la oración:

Es el Señor quien alimenta nuestra vida,
Es el Señor quien se nos da en comunión:

292　Israeli round
　　　　CH 58

Hiney mah tov umah nayim.
　shevet achim gam yachad.
(repeat)
Hiney mah tov,
　shevet achim gam yachad.
(repeat)

How good and pleasant it is
　for brothers to dwell together.
(repeat)
Good and pleasant
　for brothers to dwell together.
(repeat)

293　Omer Westendorf
　　　　CH 59

Refrain
You satisfy the hungry heart
　With gift of finest wheat;
Come give to us, O saving Lord,
　The bread of life to eat.

As when the shepherd calls his sheep,
　They know and heed his voice;
So when you call your fam'ly, Lord,
　We follow and rejoice.

With joyful lips we sing to you
　Our praise and gratitude,
That you should count us worthy, Lord,
　To share this heav'nly food.

Is not the cup we bless and share
　The blood of Christ outpoured?
Do not one cup, one loaf, declare
　Our oneness in the Lord?

The myst'ry of your presence, Lord,
　No mortal tongue can tell;
Whom all the world cannot contain
　Comes in our hearts to dwell.

You give yourself to us, O Lord;
　Then selfless let us be,
To serve each other in your name
　In truth and charity.

294　Donna Wilson
　　　　CH 60

My sheep hear my voice, I know them,
　I know them.
My sheep hear my voice, they follow me.
I give life eternal and they shall not perish;
(repeat)
　And none shall pluck them from my hand.
(repeat)

295　Anne Ortlund
　　　　CH 61

Praise God for the body,
　Praise God for the Son;
Praise God for the life
　That binds our hearts in one.

Refrain
Joy is the food we share;
　Love is our home, *brothers.
Praise God for the body;
　Shalom, shalom.

Guard your circle, *brothers,
　Clasp your hand in hand;
Satan cannot break
　The bond in which we stand.

Shed your extra clothing,
　Keep your baggage light;
Rough will be the battle,
　Long will be the fight, but:
Repeat first verse.

　　* Christians

296 Murray Davis
CH 62

*Good evening, Father,
　We delight to do your will;
*Good evening, Father,
　As we seek our hearts to fill
With the praise of your glory
　And the light of your word.
With each '*Good evening, Father,'
　We'll love you a little bit more!

Singing alleluia! Singing alleluia!
　Singing alleluia!
With each '*Good evening, Father,'
　We'll love you a little bit more!

　　* Good morning

297 Betty Pulkingham (Adapted from ICET)
CH 63

Our Father in heaven,
　Hallow'd be your name,
Your kingdom come, your will be done,
　On earth as in heaven.
Give us today our daily bread.
Forgive us our sins
　As we forgive those who sin against us.
Do not bring us to the time of trial
　But deliver us from evil.
For the kingdom, the power,
　and the glory are yours
　Now and for ever. Amen.

298 Phillip Bailey
CH 64

How much greater is the pow'r
Of the blood of Christ our Lord!
Offering himself,
　He became the living Word;
Christ the Lord, his life outpouring.

But now Christ has come to us,
　An eternal sacrifice.
Cleansing us from sin,
　He gives us new life within;
Christ the Lord, his love outpouring.

Father, we give thanks to you
　For your Son who makes us one.
By his love so free
　We become your family;
Christ the Lord, himself outpouring.

299 Kathy Wood
CH 65

Refrain
We are coming, Lord, to your table.
We are coming to eat and drink
　to remember you.

We come as one body,
　United in your spirit,
Brothers, sisters, young and old,
　To celebrate your life for us.

We come, though unworthy,
　To gather up the crumbs;
Yet healed, restored, forgiven,
　Through Jesus, who died for us.

We come rejoicing,
　With hearts for ever praising,
And lips that are singing
　Of Jesus, who lives in us.

300 vss. 1 and 2: Bill Pulkingham;
vs. 3: Martha Barker
CH 66

Refrain
Here we are, Lord, children at your feet,
　Ready to do your will.
(repeat)

Tell my people that I love them,
　Tell my people that I care;
For my peace is for them to live in,
　For my peace is for them to share.

Tell my people to share together
　All of their wealth and pain;
For my Spirit is not one of greed,
　For my Spirit is not one of shame.

Tell my people that I lead them
　As they sojourn through this land
I have gone this way before them,
　Now I guide them by my hand.

CELEBRATION

301 Beverlee Paine
CH 67

But I say unto you,
Love your enemies and pray for those
  who hurt you.
Give to those who ask, don't turn away.

Refrain
And be like your Father in heaven above
  Who causes his sun to shine
    on evil and good,
And sends down his rain to quench
    all our thirst.
  In him we live and move
    and have our being.

If you forgive each other, so will God
    forgive you.
Do not judge lest you be judged yourselves.

When you see the hungry, feed them
    from your table.
For the poor and weary,
    be their watering place.

302 Colin and Janet Lunt
CH 68

Refrain
Broken for me, broken for you;
The body of Jesus broken for you.

He offered his body, he poured out his soul;
Jesus was broken that we might be whole.

Come to my table and with me dine;
Eat of my bread and drink of my wine.

This is my body given for you;
Eat it, rememb'ring I died for you.

This is my blood I shed for you,
For your forgiveness, making you new.

303 Bill and Margi Pulkingham
CH 69

He who supplies seed to the sower
  And bread for food will supply
And multiply your resources
  And increase the harvest of righteousness.

Refrain
Praise the Lord! Let the earth rejoice.
  Praise the Lord, all ye lands!
(repeat)

Offering your service supplies the wants
  Of the saints and pleases our God.
You will be enriched in every way
  For your great generosity.

Glorify God by your obedience,
  Acknowledge the gospel of Christ.
The effect of righteousness will be peace,
  Trust, and quietness for ever.

Proclaim with your heart great thanksgiving
  For the gift of Jesus our Lord.
Belief in him gives us life eternal.
  We are one in his family.

304 Richard Gillard
CH 70

Sisters
*Brother, let me be your servant,
  Let me be as Christ to you;
Pray that I may have the grace
  To let you be my servant, too.

We are pilgrims on a journey,
  We are *brothers on the road;
We are here to help each other
  Walk the mile and bear the load.

I will hold the Christ-light for you
  In the night-time of your fear;
I will hold my hand out to you,
  Speak the peace you long to hear.

I will weep when you are weeping;
  When you laugh I'll laugh with you.
I will share your joy and sorrow
  'Til we've seen this journey through.

When we sing to God in heaven
  We shall find such harmony,
Born of all we've known together
  Of Christ's love and agony.
Repeat first verse.

  * Sister, sisters

305 Jonathan Asprey and Tim Whipple
CH 71

For our life together, we celebrate.
  Life that lasts for ever, we celebrate.
For the joy and for the sorrow,
  Yesterday, today, tomorrow, we celebrate.

For your great creation, we celebrate.
  For our own salvation, we celebrate.
For the sun and for the rain,
  Through the joy and through the pain
  we celebrate.

Ah! There's the celebration! *(3 times)*
Celebrate the whole of it!

For his body, broken, we celebrate.
  For the word he's spoken, we celebrate.
For the feasting at his table,
  By his grace we are able to celebrate.

For the Lord above, we celebrate.
  For our Father of love, we celebrate.
For the Son who is our brother,
  For his Spirit, for the three together,
  we celebrate.

Ah! There's the celebration! *(4 times)*

306   Willard F. Jabusch   CH 72

Jerusalem is fair;
  God's glory everywhere!
A home for king and peasant,
  For ages past and present.
Jerusalem is fair;
  God's glory everywhere!

How well the city shines
  With gems of many kinds;
A river through it flowing
  And treasures past all knowing.
How well the city shines
  With gems of many kinds.

Its gates will never close,
  No danger from our foes!
The saints will enter in there,
  No place for shame or sin there.
Its gates will never close,
  No danger from our foes!

God wipes all tears away,
  No death or pain can stay.
The old things now are going,
  A fresh new hope is growing.
God wipes all tears away,
  No death or pain can stay.

'Thanksgiving to the King,'
  His saints will ever sing.
Glad songs to him outpouring,
  Our Lord and Saviour adoring.
'Thanksgiving to the King,'
  His saints will ever sing.

307   Paul E. Paino   CH 73

He's able, he's able, I know he's able,
I know my Lord is able to carry me through.
(repeat)

He heals the broken-hearted,
  And sets the captive free,
He makes the lame to walk again
  And he causes the blind to see.

He's able, he's able, I know he's able,
I know my Lord is able to carry me through.

308   Author unknown   CH 74

Whosoever will to the Lord may come;
(3 times)
He'll not turn one away.

Refrain
Jesus, (Jesus), Jesus, (Jesus)
Heals the broken-hearted;
(3 times)
He will set you free.

309   Latin, 15th century (Tr. Benjamin Webb)   CH 75

O love, how deep, how broad, how high,
  How passing thought and fantasy,
That God, the Son of God, should take
  Our mortal form for mortals' sake.

For us baptised, for us he bore
  His holy fast, and hungered sore;
For us temptations sharp he knew;
  For us the tempter overthrew.

For us he preaches and he prays,
  Would do all things, would try all ways;
By words and signs and actions, thus
  Still seeking not himself, but us.

For us to wicked men betrayed,
  Scourged, mocked, in purple robe arrayed,
He bore the shameful cross and death;
  For us gave up his dying breath.

For us he rose from death again,
  For us he went on high to reign;
For us he sent his Spirit here
  To guide, to strengthen, and to cheer.

All glory to our Lord and God
  For love so deep, so high, so broad;
The trinity whom we adore
  For ever and for evermore. Amen.

CELEBRATION

310
J. H. Fillmore
CH 76

I will sing of the mercies of the Lord for ever,
   I will sing, I will sing.
I will sing of the mercies of the Lord for ever,
   I will sing of the mercies of the Lord.

With my mouth will I make known
   Thy faithfulness, thy faithfulness.
With my mouth will I make known
   Thy faithfulness to all generations.

I will sing of the mercies of the Lord for ever,
   I will sing, I will sing.
I will sing of the mercies of the Lord for ever,
   I will sing of the mercies of the Lord.

311
John B. Foley, S.J.
CH 77

Refrain
For you are my God;
You alone are my joy.
   Defend me, O Lord.

You give marvellous comrades to me:
   The faithful who dwell in your land.
Those who choose alien gods
   Have chosen an alien band.

You are my portion and cup;
   It is you that I claim for my prize.
Your heritage is my delight,
   The lot you have given to me.

Glad are my heart and my soul;
   Securely my body shall rest.
For you will not leave me for dead,
   Nor lead your beloved astray.

You show me the path for my life;
   In your presence the fullness of joy.
To be at your right hand for ever
   For me would be happiness always.

312
Thomas O. Chisholm
CH 78

Great is thy faithfulness, O God my Father,
   There is no shadow of turning with thee;
Thou changest not, thy compassions
      they fail not;
   As thou hast been thou for ever wilt be.

Refrain
Great is thy faithfulness!
   Great is thy faithfulness!
Morning by morning new mercies I see;
All I have needed thy hand hath provided –
   Great is thy faithfulness, Lord, unto me!

Summer and winter, and springtime
      and harvest,
   Sun, moon and stars in their courses above
Join with all nature in manifold witness
   To thy great faithfulness, mercy and love.

Pardon for sin and a peace that endureth,
   Thy own dear presence to cheer
      and to guide;
Strength for today and bright hope
      for tomorrow,
   Blessings all mine, with ten thousand
      beside!

313
Louise Jolly
CH 79

Awake, O sleeper, rise up from the dead.
(repeat)
   And Christ will give you light.

314
Stuart K. Hine
CH 80

O Lord my God! When I in awesome wonder
   Consider all the works thy hand hath made,
I see the stars, I hear the mighty thunder,
   Thy pow'r throughout the universe
      displayed:

Refrain
Then sings my soul, my Saviour God, to thee,
   How great thou art! How great thou art!
(repeat)

When through the woods and forest glades
      I wander,
   And hear the birds sing sweetly in the trees;
When I look down from lofty mountain
      grandeur,
   And hear the brook and feel
      the gentle breeze:

And when I think that God, his Son
      not sparing,
   Sent him to die, I scarce can take it in,
That on the cross, my burden gladly bearing,
   He bled and died to take away my sin:

When Christ shall come with shout
   of acclamation
And take me home, what joy shall fill
   my heart!
Then shall I bow in humble adoration,
   And there proclaim, my God,
      how great thou art!

315   D. W. Whittle   CH 81

I know not why God's wondrous grace
   To me hath been made known;
Nor why, unworthy as I am,
   He claimed me for his own.

Refrain
But, 'I know whom I have believed;
   And am persuaded that he is able
To keep that which I've committed
   Unto him against that day.'

I know not how this saving faith
   To me he did impart;
Or how believing in his word
   Wrought peace within my heart.

I know not how the Spirit moves,
   Convincing us of sin;
Revealing Jesus through the word,
   Creating faith in him.

I know not what of good or ill
   May be reserved for me –
Of weary ways or golden days
   Before his face I see.

I know not when my Lord may come;
   I know not how, nor where;
If I shall pass the vale of death,
   Or 'meet him in the air'.

316   Edward Mote   CH 82

My hope is built on nothing less
   Than Jesus' blood and righteousness;
I dare not trust the sweetest frame,
   But wholly lean on Jesus' name.

Refrain
On Christ the solid rock I stand;
All other ground is sinking sand,
All other ground is sinking sand.

When darkness veils his lovely face,
   I rest on his unchanging grace;
In every high and stormy gale,
   My anchor holds within the veil.

His oath, his covenant, his blood
   Support me in the whelming flood;
When all around my soul gives way
   He then is all my hope and stay.

When he shall come with trumpet sound,
   O may I then in him be found;
Dressed in his righteousness alone,
   Faultless to stand before the throne.

317   Patrick Appleford   CH 83

Lord Jesus Christ,
You have come to us,
You are one with us,
   Mary's Son.
Cleansing our souls from all their sin,
Pouring your love and goodness in,
Jesus, our love for you we sing,
   Living Lord.

*Lord Jesus Christ,
Now and every day,
Teach us how to pray,
   Son of God.
You have commanded us to do
This in remembrance, Lord, of you:
Into our lives your pow'r breaks through,
   Living Lord.

Lord Jesus Christ,
You have come to us,
Born as one of us,
   Mary's Son.
Led out to die on Calvary,
Risen from death to set us free,
Living Lord Jesus, help us see
   You are Lord.

Lord Jesus Christ,
I would come to you,
Live my life for you,
   Son of God.
All your commands I know are true,
Your many gifts will make me new,
Into my life your pow'r breaks through,
   Living Lord.

   * for Holy Communion

CELEBRATION

318
Sandy Hardyman
CH **84**

Refrain
Sing hallelujah to the Father,
 Sing hallelujah to his only Son,
 Sing praises to the Holy Spirit;
  Worship the Three in One.

In Cana the wine supply was finished,
And Jesus' mother called to him for help.
 He filled the pots with water,
 Then changed it into wine,
Just so the dance could go on.

The disciples were crossing o'er the water
And Jesus was a-sleeping in the boat.
 A fierce storm blew up
 And Jesus rose and stilled it,
Just so the dance could go on.

A sick man was lying by a pool,
Hoping that he would soon be healed.
 Jesus said, 'Arise,
 Your sins have been forgiven.
Come, and the dance will go on.'

On a hill in Jerusalem
Jesus Christ was hanged on a tree.
 He descended into hell
 And rose again to heaven,
So the dance could begin in you and me.

'Come to me as little children;
 Come, and put your hand in mine.
Come, and I will set your feet a-dancing;
 Come, and the dance goes on.'

319
Jerry Jarrett
CH **85**

When led by the Spirit, a blind man sees,
 A deaf man hears, a crippled man walks!
If I'm led by the Spirit, I will see,
 I will hear, I will walk!
God gave me his Son;
 He is the only one.
 Jesus came and he died.
But there's one thing, my friend,
 That in the very end
 Jesus rose from the dead.
All I do is believe,
All I do, all I do is believe.

When led by the Spirit, a blind man sees,
 A deaf man hears, a crippled man walks!
If you're led by the Spirit, you will see,
 You will hear, you will walk!
God gave you his Son;
 He is the only one.
 Jesus came and he died.
But there's one thing, my friend,
 That in the very end
 Jesus rose from the dead.
All you do is believe,
All you do, all you do is believe.

Lord, I was blind but now I see,
 Now I hear, now I walk!
Lord, we were blind but now we see,
 Now we hear, now we walk!
God gave us his Son;
 He is the only one.
 Jesus came and he died.
But there's one thing, my friend,
 That in the very end
 Jesus rose from the dead.
My Lord, my God, we believe,
My Lord, my God, my Lord, my God,
 we believe.

320
Robert Stoodley
CH **86**

Who | does | Jesus love,
 Jesus love, Jesus love?
Who | does | Jesus love?
 He loves everyone!

Refrain
Well, ev|'ry|body
 Should love Jesus,
  should love Jesus.
Ev|'ry|body
 Should love Jesus, too!

Who | does | Jesus care for,
 Jesus care for, Jesus care for?
Who | does | Jesus care for?
 He cares for everyone!

Refrain
Well, ev|'ry|body
 Should care for Jesus,
  should care for Jesus.
Ev|'ry|body
 Should care for Jesus, too!

Who did Jesus come to serve,
 Come to serve, come to serve?
Who did Jesus come to serve?
 He came to serve ev'ryone!

Refrain
Well, ev|'ry|body
  Should serve Jesus,
    should serve Jesus.
Ev|'ry|body
  Should serve Jesus, too!

What | did | Jesus say,
  Jesus say, Jesus say?
What | did | Jesus say?
  He said, 'Love everyone!'

Refrain
Well, ev|'ry|body
  Should love each other,
    should love each other.
Ev|'ry|body
  Should love each other, too!

Who | did | Jesus die for,
  Jesus die for, Jesus die for?
Who | did | Jesus die for?
  He died for everyone.

Refrain
Well, ev|'ry|body
  Should live for Jesus, should live for Jesus.
Ev|'ry|body
  Should live for Jesus, too!

321 Isaac Watts
CH **87**

Jesus shall reign where'er the sun
  Doth his successive journeys run;
His kingdom stretch from shore to shore,
  Till moons shall wax and wane no more.

To him shall endless prayer be made,
  And praises throng to crown his head;
His name like sweet perfume shall rise
  With every morning sacrifice.

People and realms of every tongue
  Dwell on his love with sweetest song;
And infant voices shall proclaim
  Their early blessings on his name.

Blessings abound where'er he reigns;
  The prisoner leaps to lose his chains.
The weary find eternal rest,
  And all the sons of want are blest.

Let every creature rise and bring
  Peculiar honours to our King;
Angels descend with songs again,
  And earth repeat the loud Amen.

322 Tom Colvin and friends in Ghana
CH **88**

Refrain
**Jesu, Jesu,
Fill us with your love,**
Show us how to serve
The neighbours we have from you.

Kneels at the feet of his friends,
Silently washes their feet,
Master who acts as a slave to them.

Neighbours are rich folk and poor,
Neighbours are black, brown and white,
Neighbours are nearby and far away.

These are the ones we should serve,
These are the ones we should love.
All these are neighbours to us and you.

Loving puts us on our knees,
Serving as though we were slaves,
This is the way we should live with you.

323 Frederick William Faber
CH **89**

There's a wideness in God's mercy
  Like the wideness of the sea;
There's a kindness in his justice,
  Which is more than liberty.
There is welcome for the sinner,
  And more graces for the good;
There is mercy with the Saviour;
  There is healing in his blood.

There is no place where earth's sorrows
  Are more felt than up in heav'n;
There is no place where earth's failings
  Have such kindly judgment giv'n.
There is plentiful redemption
  In the blood that has been shed;
There is joy for all the members
  In the sorrows of the Head.

For the love of God is broader
  Than the measure of man's mind;
And the heart of the Eternal
  Is most wonderfully kind.
If our love were but more simple,
  We should take him at his word;
And our lives would be all sunshine
  In the sweetness of the Lord.

CELEBRATION

324
Betty Pulkingham
CH 90

Refrain
You are my witnesses to the ends of the earth.
(repeat)

You are my people I love, gentle as dove,
Wise and harmless ones.

You are my sons of new birth, living on earth
But born from on high.

You are my trees bearing fruit
   for people to eat,
Tasting the goodness of the Lord.

You are my prophets and priests,
   proclaiming my feasts,
Telling the wonders of God.

You are my shepherds of sheep,
Over them keeping watch by night.

You are beloved of God, living his word,
Dying his death 'til he comes.

325
James Berlucchi
CH 91

All glory to the Father of life;
   Praise be to the Holy Spirit,
And to the shining light of this world.
   Jesus is the one who saves.

You're the first-born of all of the sons,
   King of the new creation.
You're the brother who makes us all one.
   Jesus is the one who saves.

Thank you, Jesus, for rising for us,
   The Father's love complete and glorious.
Now we claim the vict'ry you give to us.
   Jesus is the one who saves.

Just call upon the name of the Lord,
   Ask him for his Holy Spirit.
You'll find the one truth of this world.
   Jesus is the one who saves.

Final ending
   Jesus is the one who saves. *(repeat)*

326
Jodi Page Clark
CH 92

'**Look around you, can you see?**
   Times are troubled, people grieve.
See the violence, feel the hardness;
   All my people, weep with me.'

Refrain
Kyrie eleison,
Christe eleison,
Kyrie eleison.

'Walk among them, I'll go with you.
   Reach out to them with my hands
Suffer with me, and together
   We will serve them, help them stand.'

Forgive us, Father; hear our prayer.
   We would walk with you anywhere,
Through your suff'ring, with forgiveness,
   Take your life into the world.

327
Dave Porter
CH 93

Come! won't you come,
   For the banquet is laid.
Won't you come,
   For the feast is prepared.

Refrain
Won't you come, won't you come,
   For the banquet is laid.
Won't you come,
   For the feast is prepared.

But one man said he'd bought a house,
   Had to go and see it;
Another man said he'd bought a car,
   Had to go and try it;
While another man said he'd married a wife
   And really couldn't come;
And they all, one by one, made excuses.

But the invitation still went out
   Through the streets and alleys,
And all along the country lanes
   Where the people gathered:
'Won't you come?' And they came –
   Beggars, blind, and lame –
And they filled all the house
   where the feast was.

Jesus said, 'If you want to come with me,
Then you must love me more than your house
    or your car,
    Or even your family.
And you must love me more
    Than you love even yourself.
And where my feast is there your feast will be.'

328   Jon Polce
CH 94

Refrain
O Lord, your love is changing the world;
    Day by day we are renewed.
Your light is shining in every heart;
    The darkness will soon be consumed.

O Jesus, you are the way, the truth and life;
No one comes to the Father but by you.

O Jesus, you are the bread of life;
Feed us with your precious word.

O Jesus, you are the living water;
Fill us with eternal life.

O Jesus, we give up all our cares to you;
Lift us up upon your healing wings.

329   Kim Miller
CH 95

When the Lord came to our land,
    He was not a wealthy man.
He was born in poverty
    And the *stars* all looked to see;
And the brightest star of all was his.
Jesus was the Son of God,
    And he came to earth for me.

When the Lord came to our land,
    He was not a wealthy man.
He was born in poverty
    And the *angels* came to see;
And the angels sang their joyful news,
And the brightest star of all was his.
Jesus was the Son of God,
    And he came to earth for me.

When the Lord came to our land,
    He was not a wealthy man.
He was born in poverty
    And the *shepherds* came to see;
And the shepherds knelt and worshipped him,
And the angels sang their joyful news,
And the brightest star of all was his.
Jesus was the Son of God,
    And he came to earth for me.

When the Lord came to our land,
    He was not a wealthy man.
He was born in poverty
    And the *wise men* came to see;
And the wise men brought rare gifts for him,
And the shepherds knelt and worshipped him,
And the angels sang their joyful news,
And the brightest star of all was his.
Jesus was the Son of God,
    And he came to earth for me.

When the Lord came to our land,
    He was not a wealthy man.
He was born in poverty
    And the *donkeys* came to see;
And the donkeys gave their stall for him,
And the wise men brought rare gifts for him,
And the shepherds knelt and worshipped him,
And the angels sang their joyful news,
And the brightest star of all was his.
Jesus was the Son of God,
    And he came to earth for me.

330   B. Prout and J. Belt
CH 96

I will praise the Lord with harp and string,
    I will praise the Lord with everything;
I will praise the Lord with all my heart,
    And this is how I'll start:

Refrain
Hosanna to the living King,
    Hosanna to the Lord!
'Hosanna,' all creation sings
    To you in one accord.

I will love the Lord by loving you,
    I will love the Lord so you'll love him too;
I will love the Lord in all I do,
    For love makes all things new.

I will give the Lord the things I bear,
    I will give the Lord my every care;
For I know his love is always there.
    His praises we will share.

331   Joseph Mohr
CH 97

Silent night, holy night,
    All is calm, all is bright
Round yon virgin mother and child.
    Holy infant so tender and mild,
Sleep in heavenly peace,
    Sleep in heavenly peace.

Silent night, holy night,
  Shepherds quake at the sight,
  Glories stream from heaven afar,
  Heavenly hosts sing alleluia;
  Christ, the Saviour, is born!
    Christ, the Saviour, is born!

Silent night, holy night,
  Son of God, love's pure light
Radiant beams from thy holy face,
  With the dawn of redeeming grace,
  Jesus, Lord, at thy birth,
    Jesus, Lord, at thy birth.

332   Betty Pulkingham   CH 98

Refrain
Five barley loaves and two fishes,
  Five barley loaves and two fishes,
  Five barley loaves and two fishes,
    It was enough for him.

What are these among so many?
  What are these among so many?
  What are these among so many?
    There's not enough for them.

Give it to the Lord and he will use it.
  Give it to the Lord and he will use it.
  Give it to the Lord and he will use it.
    It's enough for him.

Took the bread and thanked his Father.
  Took the bread and thanked his Father.
  Took the bread and thanked his Father
    For the gifts he gave.

Sent it down for the people to eat.
  Sent it down for the people to eat.
  Sent it down for the people to eat
    And they were satisfied.

Twelve baskets were left over.
  Twelve baskets were left over.
  Twelve baskets were left over,
    More than enough for them!

333   Anon.; Arr. Max Dyer   CH 99

There's new life in Jesus, lift up your heart!
(repeat)
Lift up your heart! Lift up your heart!
There's new life in Jesus, lift up your heart!

Other verses may be added:
There is healing in his love, lift up your heart!
(repeat)
Lift up your heart! Lift up your heart!
There is healing in his love, lift up your heart!

There is freedom in his praise . . .

Allelu is good for you . . .

334   Swedish melody   CH 100

God is for me, though I am little;
  God is for me, though I am dumb.
God is for me, though I am lazy,
  Or mischievous or glad or glum.

Think of it: can you imagine?
  Think of it: God is for me!
Think of it: can you imagine?
  God loves even you and me!

Gud är för mig, fast jag är liten;
  Gud är för mig, fast jag är dum.
Gud är för mig, fast jag är slarvig
  Och skvallerbytta, bing, bingbång.

Tänka sig: trots alltihopa!
  Tänka sig: han är för mig.
Tänka sig: trots alltihopa!
  Han är för både dig och mig!

335   Anon.   CH 101

Peter and James and John in a sailboat,
(3 times)
Out on the beautiful sea.

They fished all night but they caught nothing,
(3 times)
Out on the beautiful sea.

Along came Jesus walkin' on the seashore,
(3 times)
Out by the beautiful sea.

He said, 'Throw your nets over on the other
  side, *(3 times)*
Out on the beautiful sea.'

The nets were filled with great big fishes,
(3 times)
Out on the beautiful sea.

The lesson of the story is listen to the Lord,
(3 times)
Wherever you may be.

336 Fiona Watson
CH 102

Refrain
We must follow the Lord in all his ways,
  Today and every single day;
We must show him that we love him,
  Our Saviour and our King.

He was born on Christmas day
  To live with a poor family.
He worked in a carpenter's shop,
  Our Saviour and our King.

He changed water into wine;
  He made the blind man see.
He healed the sick and lame,
  Our Saviour and our King.

He was nailed onto the cross
  To die for you and me.
He rose on Easter day,
  Our Saviour and our King.

He sends his spirit to us
  So that we can share his life.
He makes us one family,
  Our Saviour and our King.

337 Marie Malone
CH 103

Refrain
One must water, one must weed,
  One must sow the precious seed.
We'll all work in unity
  To tend the garden of love.

You take a little seed and put it in the ground,
  Spread a little love and cheer around.
Plant a little kindness from above
  And you'll have a garden of love.

Tend it patiently in prayer,
  Root out the weeds of doubt and care.
Trust God's spirit from above
  To nourish the seed of love.

Till the garden through and through
  As Jesus Christ directs you to.
Pour forgiveness all around
  And you'll have a fruitful ground.

338 Cecilie Hobson
CH 104

Refrain
Love you, love you, Abba, Father.
  Love you, love you, Jesus, my Lord.
  Love you, love you, gentle Spirit.
  Love you, love you, living Word.

Show me, O Father, how to be obedient,
  Putting your will before my own.

Teach me, Lord Jesus, how to be your servant,
  Part of your body here on earth.

Fill me, O Spirit, with the joy of loving,
  Giving and sharing your life in the world.

339 Sherrell Prebble
CH 105

Let us praise the Lord with guitar,
  Let us praise the Lord with guitar.
Let all the earth sing praise to the Lord,
  Let us make a joyful sound!

Other verses may be sung, e.g.
Let us praise the Lord with the tambourine

. . . piano

. . . bells.

340 Betty Pulkingham
CH 106

Refrain
Falling, falling, gently falling,
  Rain from heav'n so gently falling
On the earth, so parched and thirsty;
  God sends down his rain.

Even so, Lord, send your Spirit,
  Fall upon the poor and weary.
Those who come to you sincerely
  You'll not turn away.

'In those latter days,' the Lord says,
  'I'll pour out my Spirit on all flesh.
I shall come with power among you,
  You shall know my name.'

Even so, Lord, come among us;
  Lead and guide and purify us
In the fire of your refining,
  In the Spirit's flame.

CELEBRATION

Thank you, Jesus, Lord of heaven,
 For the gift you've freely given,
Gift of love and gift of living
 In the Spirit's power.

341 vss. 1 and 3 (alternative): Anna B. Warner
CH **107**

Jesus loves me, this I know,
 For the Bible tells me so.
Little ones to him belong.
 They are weak, but he is strong.

Refrain
Yes, Jesus loves me.
 Yes, Jesus loves me.
Yes, Jesus loves me.
 The Bible tells me so.

Jesus loves the Indian boy,
 Bow and arrow for a toy;
Big Phil'pino, wee Chinese,
 Living far across the seas.

Jesus loves the Eskimo
 In the land of ice and snow;
And he loves the cowboy, too,
 With his horse and rope lasso.

Boys and girls across the seas
 Jesus loves as well as me;
So our little friends are they,
 And with us they all can say:

Alternative verses to follow first verse.
Jesus loves me when I'm good,
 When I do the things I should.
Jesus loves me when I'm bad,
 Though it makes him very sad.

Jesus loves me, he who died,
 Heaven's gates to open wide.
He will wash away my sin,
 Let this little child come in.

342 Ghana work song (Tr. Tom Colvin)
CH **108**

(leader) **Christ the worker,**
 (all) Christ the worker,
  Born in Bethlehem,
  Born to work and die
   for everyone.

(leader) Blessed manchild,
 (all) Blessed manchild,
  Boy of Nazareth,
  Grew in wisdom
   as he grew in skill.

(leader) Skilful craftsman,
 (all) Skilful craftsman,
  Blessed carpenter,
  Praising God by labour
   at his bench.

(leader) Yoke maker,
 (all) Yoke maker,
  Fashioned by his hands,
  Easy yokes that make
   the labour less.

(leader) You who labour,
 (all) You who labour,
  Listen to his call,
  He will make that heavy
   burden light.

(leader) Heavy laden,
 (all) Heavy laden,
  Gladly come to him,
  He will ease your load
   and give you rest.

(leader) Christ the worker,
 (all) Christ the worker,
  Love alive for us,
  Teach us how to do
   all work for God.

343 Alex Simons and Freda Kimmey
CH **109**

God is our Father,
 For he has made us his *own.
Made Jesus our brother,
 And hand in hand we grow together as one.

Sing praise to the Lord with tambourine.
 Sing praise to the Lord with clapping hands.
Sing praise to the Lord with dancing feet.
 Sing praise to the Lord with our voice:

La la la la la la
 la la la la . . .

 * *original:* sons

344 Phil Higgs
CH **110**

Refrain
**O Lord, our Lord, how great is your name
 in the earth.**
(repeat)

In the mouths of babes you establish praise.
Nations of the world end their warring days.

I see the heav'ns, the work of your hand;
You placed the moon and stars
   according to your plan.

What is man that you should care for him?
You crowned him with glory
   and made him a king.

You made him rule all the works of your hand,
And put everything | at his command.

345   Merla Watson
CH 111

The Lord's my shepherd, I'll not want.
   He makes me down to lie
In pastures green: he leadeth me
   The quiet waters by.
My soul he doth restore again;
   And me to walk doth make
Within the paths of righteousness,
   E'en for his own name's sake.

Yea, though I walk in death's dark vale,
   Yet will I fear none ill:
For thou art with me, and thy rod
   And staff me comfort still.
My table thou hast furnished
   In presence of my foes;
My head thou dost with oil anoint,
   And my cup overflows.

Goodness and mercy all my life
   Shall surely follow me:
And in God's house for evermore
   My dwelling place shall be.
Hallelujah, hallelujah,
   Hallelujah, hallelujah!
Hallelujah, hallelujah,
   Hallelujah, amen!

346   Shirley Lewis Brown
CH 112

The Lord is my light and my salvation;
   Whom then shall I fear?
The Lord is the strength of my life;
   Of whom shall I be afraid?

347   Mike Fitzgerald
CH 113

Refrain
Israel, rely on Yahweh
Now and for evermore.

Yahweh, my heart is not ambitious.
My eyes do not look too high.

I am not concerned with greatness
Or marvels beyond my scope.

Enough for me to keep my soul tranquil
Like a child in its mother's arms,
   As content as a child that has been weaned.

Glory be to the Father Almighty,
To the Son and Spirit praise,
   Eternal praise in endless peace.

348   Old Round
CH 114

The Lord is my shepherd,
   my needs are provided;
I rest in green pastures beside the still waters.

He strengthens my spirit;
   I walk without fearing,
For he is beside me to guide and protect me.

My table is spread where his peace
   is around me;
He soothes me with oil, and my cup runneth
   over.

Surely /goodness and love
   will ever be with me,
And I shall abide in his presence for ever.

349   John Smith
CH 115

Those who trust in the Lord
   Are like Mount Zion
Which shall never be removed,
   And shall remain for ever.

As the mountains are about,
   Are about Jerusalem,
So the Lord is 'round about,
   'Round his people here.

Peace be on Israel,
   Peace be on Israel,
Peace be on Israel
   Now and for evermore.

Alleluia, allelu,
   Alleluia, allelu,
Alleluia, allelu,
   Alleluia.

CELEBRATION

350
Linda Spencer
CH 116

Refrain
Sing unto the Lord, sing a new song,
 Sing unto him.
Sing unto the Lord, all the earth.
Sing unto the Lord, bless his name,
 Sing unto him.
Sing unto the Lord, sing a new song.

For the Lord is great
 And greatly to be praised.
We lift our hearts,
 And with our voices praise.

Give unto the Lord
 All the glory due his name;
For his love he's shown,
 And to the earth he came.

Let the heav'ns rejoice
 And let the earth be glad;
For he comes again,
 And a new song we now have.

351
Gail Cole and Glenn Cummings
CH 117

Refrain
I will dwell in his secret place;
 In his shadow I will abide.
In his fortress I will take refuge,
 In my God, the Most High.

From plague and from snare
  you are protected;
 You need not fear the dark of night.
And with his wing you will be covered,
 Delivered from the wicked's might.

There shall no evil o'ercome you,
 Neither shall the plague come nigh;
For he shall place his angels o'er you
 To keep you safe in all your ways.

When I call to the Lord he will answer.
 He will set my soul on high.
He will be near in time of trouble,
 Give long life, and satisfy.

352
Fred Dunn
CH 118

Jubilate, everybody,
 Serve the Lord in all your ways, and
Come before his presence singing;
 Enter now his courts with praise.
For the Lord our God is gracious,
 And his mercy everlasting.
Jubilate, jubilate, jubilate Deo!

353
Refrain: Hugh Mitchell;
Verses: Jan Harrington
CH 119

Refrain
Thy lovingkindness is better than life,
 Thy lovingkindness is better than life.
My lips shall praise thee; thus will I bless thee:
 I will lift up my hands in thy name.

Early will I seek thee, O God, thou art my God;
 Early will I seek thee, O God,
  thou art my God.
My soul thirsteth for thee,
 my flesh longeth for thee
In a thirsty land where no water is.

So I come before thee, O God,
  thou art my God;
 So I come before thee, O God,
  thou art my God;
So I come to thy house to see thy power
  and thy glory,
 And my soul is satisfied.

When I remember and meditate on thee;
 When I remember and meditate on thee,
I rejoice. In the shadow of thy wings
  will I rejoice
Because thy right hand upholdeth me.

*If the refrain is used without the verses, it may
be lengthened (by repetition) to the words:*
I lift my hands up unto thy name,
 I lift my hands up unto thy name.
My lips shall praise thee, thus will I bless thee,
 I will lift up my hands in thy name.

354
Jonathan Asprey
CH 120

Refrain
O be joyful in the Lord! *(repeat)*
 Let us make a joyful noise,
 Let the whole earth rejoice!
O be joyful in the Lord, all ye lands!

Know that the Lord he is God:
 He has made us, we are his.
We are the sheep of his pasture,
 The people of his hand.

Enter his gates with thanksgiving:
 Come into his courts with praise.
Be thankful unto him,
 And speak good of his name.

Know that the Lord he is good:
 His love lasts for ever.
He's faithful and true
 Through every generation.

355 Graeme Wise
CH 121

Come and bless the Lord,
All you who serve him,
Who stand night after night
In the house of the Lord.
Lift up your hands in the sanctuary
And bless the Lord.
The Lord, the maker of heav'n and earth,
Bless you from Zion;
The Lord, the maker of heav'n and earth,
Bless you from Zion.

356 Tim Manion
CH 122

Refrain
To you, Yahweh, I lift up my soul, O my God.
(repeat)

Yahweh, show your ways to me.
Teach me your paths
And keep me in the ways of your truth,
For you are the God that saves me.

The Lord is so good, so holy,
Sinners find the way,
And in all that is right he guides the humble.
The poor he leads in his pathways.

All day long I hope in your goodness,
Remember your love,
The love that you promised long ago,
And the kindness that you gave from of old.

357 Michelle Stoodley
CH 123

Refrain
Lift up your heads, O ye gates,
And be lifted up, O ancient doors,
That the King of Glory may come in.
(repeat)

The earth is the Lord's and the fullness thereof,
The world and those who dwell therein.
He has founded it upon the seas
And has established it upon the rivers.

Who shall ascend the hill of the Lord
And stand in his holy place?
He who has clean hands and a pure heart,
Who does not lift up his soul to what is false.

The blessing of the Lord is theirs
And peace from the God of their salvation.
Such is the people who seek him,
Who seek the face of the God of Jacob.

Who is the King of Glory?
The Lord strong and mighty in battle.
Who is this King of Glory?
The Lord of hosts is his name.

358 Arr. Jonathan Asprey
CH 124

How lovely is thy dwelling-place,
O Lord of hosts, to me.
My soul is longing and fainting
The courts of the Lord to see.
My heart and flesh, they are singing
For joy to the living God.
How lovely is thy dwelling-place,
O Lord of hosts, to me.

Even the sparrow finds a home
Where he can settle down.
And the swallow, she can build a nest
Where she may lay her young
Within the courts of the Lord of hosts,
My King, my Lord, and my God.
And happy are those who are dwelling where
The song of praise is sung.

And I'd rather be a door-keeper
And only stay a day,
Than live the life of a sinner
And have to stay away.
For the Lord is shining as the sun,
And the Lord, he's like a shield;
And no good thing does he withhold
From those who walk his way.
Repeat first verse.

359 Latin, 9th century (Tr. John Cosin)
CH 125

Come, Holy Ghost, our souls inspire,
And lighten with celestial fire;
Thou the anointing Spirit art,
Who dost thy sevenfold gifts impart.

Thy blessed unction from above
Is comfort, life, and fire of love;
Enable with perpetual light
The dullness of our blinded sight.

Anoint and cheer our soiled face
With the abundance of thy grace:
Keep far our foes, give peace at home;
Where thou art guide no ill can come.

CELEBRATION

Teach us to know the Father, Son,
   And thee, of Both, to be but One;
That through the ages all along
   This may be our endless song,
'Praise to thy eternal merit,
   Father, Son, and Holy Spirit.'

360   Charles Wesley
        CH 126

Christ the Lord is ris'n today, Alleluia!
   Sons of men and angels say, Alleluia!
Raise your joys and triumphs high, Alleluia!
   Sing, ye heav'ns, and earth reply, Alleluia!

Lives again our glorious King; Alleluia!
   Where, O death, is now thy sting? Alleluia!
Once he died our souls to save, Alleluia!
   Where thy victory, O grave? Alleluia!

Love's redeeming work is done, Alleluia!
   Fought the fight, the battle won, Alleluia!
Death in vain forbids him rise, Alleluia!
   Christ has opened paradise, Alleluia!

Soar we now where Christ has led, Alleluia!
   Following our exalted Head, Alleluia!
Made like him, like him we rise, Alleluia!
   Ours the cross, the grave, the skies, Alleluia!

361   David McKeithen
        CH 127

Good morning, this is the day, *(3 times)*
   Which the Lord has made.

We will rejoice and be glad, *(3 times)*
   Lift up our hands and praise his name.

Christ is risen today. *(3 times)*
   Alleluia, alleluia!

362   Latin, 13th century
        CH 128

At the cross her station keeping,
Stood the mournful mother weeping,
   Where he hung, the dying Lord:
For her soul of joy bereaved,
Bowed with anguish, deeply grieved,
   Felt the sharp and piercing sword.

O how sad and sore distressed
Now was she, that mother blessed
   Of the sole-begotten One.

Deep the woe of her affliction,
When she saw the crucifixion
   Of her ever-glorious Son.

Who, on Christ's dear mother gazing,
Pierced by anguish so amazing,
   Born of woman, would not weep?
Who, on Christ's dear mother thinking,
Such a cup of sorrow drinking,
   Would not share her sorrows deep?

For his people's sins chastised,
She beheld her Son despised,
   Scourged, and crowned with thorns
     entwined;
Saw him then from judgment taken,
And in death by all forsaken,
   Till his spirit he resigned.

Jesus, may her deep devotion
Stir in me the same emotion,
   Fount of love, Redeemer kind;
That my heart fresh ardour gaining,
And a purer love attaining,
   May with thee acceptance find. Amen.

363   Philipp Bliss
        CH 129

'Man of sorrows', what a name
For the Son of God, who came
Ruin'd sinners to reclaim!
   Hallelujah! what a Saviour!

Bearing shame and scoffing rude,
In my place condemned he stood;
Sealed my pardon with his blood:
   Hallelujah! what a Saviour!

Guilty, vile, and helpless, we;
Spotless Lamb of God was he:
'Full atonement', can it be?
   *Hallelujah! what a Saviour!

Lifted up was he to die,
'It is finished!' was his cry.
Now in heav'n exalted high:
   Hallelujah! what a Saviour!

When he comes, our glorious King,
All his ransomed home to bring,
Then anew this song we'll sing:
   'Hallelujah! what a Saviour!'

   * *In stanzas 3, 4 and 5 'Hallelujah' may be repeated (even twice) as the sense of exultation grows.*

364
Charles Wesley
CH **130**

Lo! he comes, with clouds descending,
  Once for our salvation slain;
Thousand, thousand saints attending
  Swell the triumph of his train.
    Alleluia, *(4 times)*
  Christ the Lord returns to reign.

Every eye shall now behold him,
  Robed in dreadful majesty;
Those who set at naught and sold him,
  Pierced and nailed him to the tree,
    Deeply wailing, *(4 times)*
  Shall the true Messiah see.

Those dear tokens of his passion
  Still his dazzling body bears;
Cause of endless exultation
  To his ransomed worshippers.
    With what rapture *(4 times)*
  Gaze we on those glorious scars.

Yea, amen! Let all adore thee,
  High on thine eternal throne;
Saviour, take the power and glory;
  Claim the kingdom for thine own:
    Alleluia, *(4 times)*
  Thou shalt reign, and thou alone.

365
Traditional
CH **131**

Dona nobis pacem, pacem.
  Dona nobis pacem.

Dona nobis pacem.
  Dona nobis pacem.

Dona nobis pacem.
  Dona nobis pacem.

366
Mimi Farra
CH **132**

Refrain
We cry, 'Hosanna, Lord,'
  Yes, 'Hosanna, Lord,'
    Yes, 'Hosanna, Lord,' to you.
(repeat)

Behold, our Saviour comes.
  Behold the Son of our God.
He offers himself and he comes among us,
  A lowly servant to all.

Children wave their palms as the
  King of all kings rides by.
Should we forget to praise our God,
  The very stones would sing.

He comes to set us free.
  He gives us liberty.
His vict'ry over death
  Is the eternal sign of God's love for us.

367
Diane Davis Andrew
CH **133**

Refrain
I will pour out my Spirit upon all flesh. *(repeat)*
  Cry out to the nations;
  Tell them I have promised
I will pour out my Spirit upon all flesh.

Your sons and your daughters will prophesy,
  Your young men shall see visions,
Your old men will dream dreams.
  In those days I will pour out my Spirit.

All mankind will know me;
  They will call me by my name.
I will live among them,
  Teaching them to walk in my ways.

Come and see the signs I give,
  Darkened sun, moon to blood.
Behold I am the Lord your God;
  Is anything too hard for me?

368
Maggie Durran
CH **134**

Refrain
Here he comes, robed in majesty,
  King of the Jews,
Living with power among us.
  He's won the vict'ry over death.

Come behold the King, Jesus, risen Son,
  Offering his life to us all.
Come receive his life of sacrifice;
  Come taste his flesh and his blood.
And God sends down love.

Come behold the life, Spirit of the Lord,
  Offering his pow'r to us all,
As at Pentecost
  When the Spirit drew the ones
    whom Jesus loved,
And God sent down fire.

Come among us now, Jesus, risen Lord,
    Offering the grace for unity.
Christ is in our midst;
    We're abandoned to the fullness of his life.
And God sends down pow'r.

369   William B. Carpenter   CH 135

Before thy throne, O God, we kneel;
    Give us a conscience quick to feel,
A ready mind to understand
    The meaning of thy chast'ning hand;
Whate'er the pain and shame may be,
    Bring us, O Father, nearer thee.

Search out our hearts and make us true,
    Wishful to give to all their due;
From love of pleasure, lust of gold,
    From sins which make the heart grow cold,
Wean us and train us with thy rod;
    Teach us to know our faults, O God.

For sins of heedless word and deed,
    For pride ambitious to succeed,
For crafty trade and subtle snare
    To catch the simple unaware,
For lives bereft of purpose high,
    Forgive, forgive, O Lord, we cry.

Let the fierce fires which burn and try,
    Our inmost spirits purify:
Consume the ill; purge out the shame;
    O God, be with us in the flame;
A newborn people may we rise,
    More pure, more true, more nobly wise.
        Amen.

370   Eric Glass   CH 136

Behold, the darkness shall cover the earth,
    And gross darkness the people;
But the Lord shall arise upon thee,
    And his glory shall be seen upon thee.

Refrain
Arise, shine; for thy light is come,
    And the glory of the Lord is risen.
Oh, arise, shine; for thy light is come,
    And the glory of the Lord is upon thee.

The gentiles shall come to thy light,
    And kings to the brightness of thy rising.
And they shall call thee 'the city of the Lord,
    The Zion of the Holy One of Israel'.

Lift up thine eyes round about and see,
    They gather themselves together.
And they shall come, thy sons from afar,
    And thy daughters shall be nursed
        at thy side.

Then shalt thou see and flow together,
    And thy heart shall be enlarged;
The abundance of the sea is converted
        unto thee,
    And the nations shall come unto thee.

The sun shall no more go down,
    Neither shall the moon withdraw itself;
But the Lord shall be thine everlasting light,
    And the days of thy mourning shall be
        ended.

371   Wiley Beveridge and Glenna J. McLane   CH 137

In the little town of Bethlehem long ago
A little babe was born to save
    the world from all woe.

Refrain
How the angels sang, 'Allelu.'
Sing to Jesus, sing, 'Allelu.'

In a manger lay this babe of love
    through the night.
The shepherds came in joy and haste
    to see God's own light.

Refrain
How the shepherds sang, 'Allelu.'
Sing to Jesus, sing, 'Allelu.'

Wise men, ox and ass, come join the praise
    of his birth.
Children of the light proclaim good news
    to the earth.

Refrain
Lift your voices, sing, 'Allelu.'
Sing to Jesus, sing, 'Allelu.'

Final ending
'Allelu, allelu, allelu.'

372   Laura Winnen   CH 138

Refrain
My Lord, he is a-comin' soon;
    Prepare ye the way of the Lord.
Get everything ready for that day;
    Prepare ye the way of the Lord.

If you're asleep, it's time to wake up;
   Awake, O sleeper, arise.
If you're in the dark, it's time to be lit;
   Awake, O sleeper, arise!

Come, Lord Jesus, come into my heart;
   Prepare ye the way of the King.
He is coming, he's coming soon;
   Prepare the way of the King!

373   Colleen O'Meara   CH 139

Sing a song, a joyful song,
   Sing unto the Lord.
Sing a song, a joyful song,
   Sing unto the Lord.

Refrain
Clap your hands, all you people,
   Clap your hands unto the Lord.
Dance your feet, all you people,
   Dance unto the Lord.

See the baby in a manger,
   See the baby softly sleeping,
See the baby in a manger:
   Come with me and see.

See the mother rock the baby,
   Rock the baby, rock the baby,
See the mother rock the baby:
   Come with me and see.

Hear the donkey hee and hawing,
   Hee and hawing, hee and hawing,
Hear the donkey hee and hawing:
   Come with me and see.

Shepherds on the hills a-watching,
   Hills a-watching, hills a-watching,
Shepherds on the hills a-watching:
   Come with me and see.

See the star so brightly shining,
   Brightly shining, brightly shining,
See the star so brightly shining:
   Come with me and see.

Kings upon their camels riding,
   Camels riding, camels riding,
Kings upon their camels riding,
   Bringing gifts to him.

374   Jodi Page Clark   CH 140

Cradle rocking, cattle lowing,
   Bright star guiding men to see
Little Christ-child in the manger;
   Light of all the world to be.

Refrain
Hallelujah, holy child.
   Hosanna in the highest.
Gloria, Emmanuel.
   Hosanna in the highest.

Mother Mary, watching carefully
   By the light of one bright star
Bread of heaven, softly sleeping,
   Gentle gift of God to us.

Who could guess, to see you lie there,
   That you came to bring a sword?
Prince of peace, upon the manger,
   With a price upon your soul.

Do you know, so weak and helpless,
   Of the grace you bear to us?
Do you dream yet of the kingdom
   You will some day bring to pass?

375   Kiko Argüello (Tr. Susan Abbott)   CH 141

Refrain
¡**Resucitó, resucitó,** resucitó, aleluya!
¡Aleluya, aleluya, aleluya, resucitó!

Death, where is death?
Where is its sting? Where is its vict'ry?

Rejoice and be happy together.
If we love each other it's because he is risen.

If with him we die, with him we live,
With him we sing: 'Alleluia.'

376   John Richards   CH 142

Spirit, working in creation,
   Bringing order out of strife:
Come around God's gathered people,
   Giving harmony and life.

Spirit, speaking through the prophets
   So the voice of God was heard:
Come, inspire, alert your people
   To today's prophetic word.

CELEBRATION

Spirit, overshadowing Mary
   As the Christ-child in her grew:
Come, so that the Christ within us
   May today be born anew.

Spirit, coming from the Father
   As a dove upon our Lord:
Come upon your favoured people
   And your blessings be outpoured.

Spirit, driving to the desert
   Even God's Anointed One:
Come to us in trial and testing
   That God's will in us be done.

Spirit, bringing freedom, blessing,
   Help to poor, and health to lame:
Come, anoint us, that such wonders
   May be done in Jesus' Name.

*Spirit, taking, breaking, making
   Bread and wine our heavenly food:
Come, and take us, break us, make us,
   Live Christ's life in us renewed.

Spirit, breathed on the disciples,
   Giving peace where there was fear:
Come amongst us, touch us, send us,
   Making Jesus' presence near.

Spirit, wind and flame, empow'ring
   Fearless witness to the lost:
Come, unite, 'renew your wonders
   As of a new Pentecost!'

Praise and glory, Holy Spirit,
   For your love on us outpoured:
Giving honour to the Father,
   And proclaiming Jesus – Lord.

   * *for Holy Communion*

COPYRIGHT HOLDERS
(listed by song number)

Full details of Copyright Acknowledgements are given in the Music Editions of 'Sound of Living Waters', 'Fresh Sounds' and 'Cry Hosanna'

1 © 1973, The Word of God
2 © 1967, 1970, American Catholic Press
7 © 1974, 1975, Celebration
8 © 1974, 1975, Celebration
9 © David Higham Associates
10 © 1967, Sacred Songs/Word Music Inc.
12 © Josef Weinberger Ltd.
13 © Les Garrett
15 © 1972, G.I.A. Publications, Inc.
19 © 1972, Lexicon Music, Inc.
20 © Gospel Publishing House
21 © 1971, 1975, Celebration
26 © 1972, Maranatha! Music
28 © Fred Bock Music Co.
29 © 1935, 1963, Moody Press
31 © 1974, Sylvia Lawton
33 © 1970, 1975, Celebration
38 © 1958, Gospel Publishing House
42 © 1951, Mrs H. Head
44 © Jan Struther
51 © 1974, David Lynch
52 © 1974, Pamela Greenwood
54 © 1974, Alan D. Teage
55 © 1973, Maranatha! Music
56 © 1973, Maranatha! Music
57 © 1971, 1975, Celebration
59 © 1973, 1975, Celebration
64 © Dawn Treader Music
66 © 1974, 1975, Celebration
70 © 1971, 1975, Celebration
73 © 1950, Singspiration, Inc.
73 © 1971, 1975, Celebration
74 © 1949, Zondervan Publishers
78 © 1971, Springtide/Word Music (UK) Ltd.
80 © 1973, The Word of God
82 © 1971, 1975, Celebration
86 © 1965, Josef Weinberger Ltd.
89 © 1969, Vanguard Music Corp.
91 © W. F. Jabusch
92 © 1964, J. E. Seddon & M. A. Baughen
94 © 1971, 1975, Celebration
99 © 1974, Timothy Dudley-Smith
102 © 1974, 1975, Celebration
103 © 1974, 1975, Celebration
106 © 1971, Elizabeth Syré
107 © 1971, 1975, Celebration
108 © 1974, 1975, Celebration
109 © 1971, 1975, Celebration
110 © 1974, 1975, Celebration
111 © 1965, Vanguard Music Corp.
112 © 1972, 1975, Celebration
114 © 1969, M. Perry & S. Coates

115 © 1973, G.I.A. Publications, Inc.
118 © 1974, 1975, Celebration
120 © W. F. Jabusch
121 © 1972, G.I.A. Publications, Inc.
125 (refrain) © 1912, 1940, Hope Publishing Co.
125 (verses) © 1971, 1975, Celebration
127 © 1974, G.I.A. Publications Inc.
129 © 1974, 1975, Celebration
132 © 1967, The Cameron Brothers Revivals and Roy Turner
133 © 1975, Celebration
134 © 1973, G.I.A. Publications, Inc.
135 © 1967, The Cameron Brothers Revivals and Roy Turner
137 © 1973, 1975, The Word of God
138 © 1973, G.I.A. Publications, Inc.
139 © 1974, The Word of God
140 © 1975, Celebration
141 © 1975, Church of the Messiah
142 © 1974, Celebration
143 © 1971, 1975, Celebration
145 © 1970, 1975, Celebration
147 © 1948, John Ireland
148 © 1970, 1975, Celebration
150 © 1973, G.I.A. Publications, Inc.
152 © 1962, Gospel Publishing House
156 © 1922, 1950, Singspiration, Inc.
159 © 1972, G.I.A. Publications, Inc.
160 © 1971, 1975, Celebration
161 © 1972, Youth With A Mission, Inc.
162 © 1975, Celebration
163 © 1975, Celebration
164 © 1973, G.I.A. Publications, Inc.
165 © 1975, Celebration
167 © International Consultation on English Texts
168 © 1955, Shari Music Publishing Co.
168 (verse 2) © 1975, Celebration
170 © 1972, Lexicon Music Inc.
171 © International Consultation on English Texts
173 © 1974, 1975, Celebration
174 © 1975, Celebration
176 © 1971, 1975, Celebration
177 © 1969, Intervarsity Press
178 © 1974, 1975, Celebration
179 © Brian Casebow
180 © 1972, G.I.A. Publications, Inc.

181 © 1975, Celebration
182 © 1975, Celebration
183 © Inter-Varsity Christian Fellowship of U.S.A.
184 © 1973, G.I.A. Publications, Inc.
185 © 1970, Inter-Lutheran Commission on Worship
186 © 1975, Celebration
188 © 1975, Church of the Messiah
189 © 1975, Celebration
190 © 1974, 1975, Celebration
191 © Delys S. Webb
192 Elinor Fosdick Fowns
193 © 1973, 1975, Celebration
194 © 1974, 1975, Celebration
195 © 1974, Clint Taylor and the Church of the Good Shepherd
196 © 1974, 1975, Celebration
198 © 1975, Olwen Wonnacott
199 © 1975, Mary Ackroyd
200 (verses) © 1974, 1975, Celebration
201 © 1974, 1975, Celebration
202 © 1957, Singspiration, Inc.
206 © M. Baughen
209 © 1971, Ann House
210 © 1974, 1975, Celebration
211 Morehouse-Barlow Co.
212 © 1971, 1975, Celebration
213 © 1975, Celebration
214 © 1974, 1975, Celebration
215 © 1971, 1975, Celebration
218 © 1971, 1975, Celebration
219 © 1971, 1975, Celebration
221 © 1973, Robert Reynolds
223 Franciscan Communications Centre
224 © 1974, 1975, The Word of God
225 © 1971, 1975, Celebration
226 © 1955, Jan-Lee Music
227 © 1972, Lexicon Music (UK)
228 © 1969, 1971, 1973, North American Liturgy Resources
230 © 1973, St Paul's Outreach Trust
231 © 1975, Celebration
233 © 1969, Jim Strathdee
234 © 1974, 1975, Celebration
235 © 1975, Celebration
236 © 1974, Reba Place Fellowship
238 © 1974, Wiley Beveridge
239 © 1974, 1982 Celebration
240 © 1975, Celebration
241 © 1978, Sparrow Song/Candle Company Music
242 © 1975, Church of the Messiah
243 © 1977, Celebration
245 © 1974, The Word of God
247 © 1973, Concordia Publishing House
248 © 1978, Celebration
249 © 1979, Celebration
250 © 1977, Celebration

CELEBRATION

- 251 © 1973, 1982, Celebration
- 253 © 1962, Timothy Dudley-Smith
- 254 © 1977, Scripture in Song
- 255 © 1973, 1975, Celebration
- 256 International Consultation on English Texts
- 257 © 1977, Celebration
- 258 © 1972, Scripture in Song
- 259 © 1976, Church of the Messiah
- 260 © 1978, Mustard Seed Music
- 261 © 1974, 1982, Celebration
- 263 © 1975, St Paul's Outreach Trust
- 264 © 1975, Celebration
- 266 © 1974, 1975, Celebration
- 267 © 1978, Mustard Seed Music
- 268 © 1974, 1978, Scripture in Song
- 269 © 1959, Manna Music, Inc.
- 270 © 1979, Martha Butler
- 271 © 1973, Hope Publishing Company
- 272 © 1975, Celebration
- 273 © 1969, 1971, 1975, North American Liturgy Resources
- 276 © 1978, Celebration
- 277 © 1973, G.I.A. Publications, Inc.
- 278 © 1979, John McNeil
- 279 © 1959, 1964, Sacred Songs/Word, Inc.
- 280 © 1953, Hamblen Music Co.
- 281 © 1974, 1975, Celebration
- 283 © 1975, Celebration
- 284 (refrain) © 1972, Gospel Publishing House
- 284 (verses) © 1975, Celebration
- 285 © 1973, G.I.A. Publications, Inc.
- 286 © 1978, Celebration
- 287 © 1975, Celebration
- 288 © 1975, St Paul's Outreach Trust
- 289 © 1978, Celebration
- 290 © LeRoy Pratt Percy
- 291 © 1968, Bonum Editorial
- 293 © 1976, 41st International Eucharist Congress, Inc.
- 294 © 1978, Donna Wilson Lakos
- 295 © 1970, Singspiration, Inc.
- 296 © Christ's Community
- 297 © International Consultation on English Texts
- 298 © 1978, Redeemer Baptist Church
- 299 © 1975, Kathy Wood Thompson
- 300 © 1978, Celebration
- 301 © 1979, Celebration
- 302 © 1978, Mustard Seed Music
- 303 © 1977, Celebration
- 304 © 1977, Scripture in Song
- 305 © 1975, Celebration
- 306 © 1974, W. F. Jabusch
- 307 © 1958, Singspiration, Inc.
- 311 © 1970, John B. Foley and North American Liturgy Resources
- 312 © 1923, 1951, Hope Publishing Co.
- 313 © 1975, Celebration
- 314 © 1953, Manna Music Ltd
- 317 © 1960, Josef Weinberger Ltd.
- 318 © 1978, Celebration
- 319 © 1976, Alleluia Community (God Unlimited)
- 320 © 1978, Mustard Seed Music
- 322 © 1969, Agape
- 324 © 1975, Celebration
- 325 © 1974, The Word of God
- 326 © 1976, Celebration
- 327 © 1977, Celebration
- 328 © 1979, Jon Polce
- 329 © 1977, Parish of Eastbourne Trust Board
- 330 © 1976, Álleluia Community (God Unlimited)
- 332 © 1971, 1975, Celebration
- 333 © 1977, Celebration
- 336 © 1978, Mustard Seed Music
- 337 © 1977, Church of the Redeemer
- 338 © 1978, Celebration
- 339 © 1975, Celebration
- 340 © 1972, 1975, Celebration
- 342 © 1969, Agape
- 343 © 1977, Celebration
- 344 © 1977, Celebration
- 345 © Gordon V. Thompson Limited
- 346 © 1978, Celebration
- 347 © 1974, The Word of God
- 349 © 1974, St Paul's Outreach Trust
- 350 © 1971, Linda Spencer
- 351 © 1975, Church of the Messiah
- 352 © 1978, 1980, Thankyou Music
- 353 (refrain) © 1956, Singspiration Inc.
- 353 (verses) © 1975, Celebration
- 354 © 1976, Celebration
- 355 © 1975, St Paul's Outreach Trust
- 356 © 1976, Tim Manion and North American Liturgy Resources
- 357 © 1978, Mustard Seed Music
- 358 © 1975, Celebration
- 361 © 1978, Sojourners, People's Christian Coalition
- 362 © 1979, Celebration
- 364 © 1976, Celebration
- 366 © 1975, Celebration
- 367 © 1976, Celebration
- 368 © 1976, Celebration
- 370 © 1974, Eric Glass
- 371 © 1973, 1982, Celebration
- 372 © 1975, Celebration
- 373 © 1976, Celebration
- 374 © 1975, Celebration
- 375 © 1972, Francisco Gómez Argüello
- 376 © 1978, John Richards

INDEX OF TITLES AND FIRST LINES

The title of a song is included, in italic type, only where it differs from the first line.

A joyful song	373
A new commandment	63
Abba, Father	338
Alabaré	238
All glory to the Father of life	325
All the riches of his grace	264
Allelu	160
Allelu, 'lu-ia, 'lu-ia	287
Alleluia	25
Alleluia! Alleluia!	82
Alleluia, alleluia, give thanks	1
Alleluia! Alleluia! Opening our hearts to him	289
Alleluia, he is coming	270
Alleluia No. 1	1
Alleluia! Sing to Jesus	53
Alleluia! Sons of God, arise!	82
Amazing grace	5
And can it be	81
And ye shall have power	230
Angel voices ever singing	12
Anyone who does the will of God	188
Arise, shine!	370
As a doe	97
Ask, and it shall be given you	212
At the cross	62
At the cross her station keeping	362
At the name of Jesus	44
Awake, awake to love and work	282
Awake, O sleeper	313
Ballad of the dance	318
Be like your Father	301
Before the Lord Jehovah's throne	247
Before thy throne, O God	369
Behold, how good and how pleasant it is	94
Behold, the darkness shall cover the earth	370
Bell song, The	51
Bethlehem song	371
Bless the holy name of Jesus	266
Bless thou the Lord	100
Bless you, Jesus	221
Blessed be the name	149
Blessing and honour	256
Blow, thou cleansing wind	54
Body song, The	107
Bridegroom's song, The	278
Broken for me	302
Brother, let me be your servant	304
But I say unto you	301
Butterfly song, The	102
By their fruits ye shall know them	180
By your stripes	52
Calypso carol	114
Calypso Doxology	168
Can men gather grapes from the thorns	180
Canticle of the gift, The	2
Celebration song, The	305
Children at your feet	300
Christ the Lord is risen today (SLW)	124
Christ the Lord is risen today (CH)	360
Christ the worker	342
Christmas lullaby	374
Clap your hands	250
Clean hands	220
Come and bless	160
Come and bless the Lord	355
Come and go with me	83
Come follow me now	234
Come go with me to that land	204
Come, Holy Ghost	359
Come, Holy Ghost creator blest	126
Come into his presence	146
Come, Lord Jesus	281
Come to the waters	231
Come with me to a land where people are free	215
Come! won't you come	327
Come, ye sinners, poor and needy	274
Comfort ye	195
Complete in him	72
Cradle rocking, cattle lowing	374
Crown him with many crowns	130
Dancing heart, The	135
David danced before the Lord	135
Day by day	36 & 37
Dear Lord and Father of mankind	50
Dona nobis pacem	365
Doxology	170
Drop everything and go	225
Everybody song	320
Faith is the victory	200
Falling, falling, gently falling	340
Father, we adore you	26
Fear not, for I have redeemed you	283
Fear not, rejoice and be glad	57
Fight the good fight	198
Fill my cup, Lord	279
Fill your heart with love	251
Fishermen, The	290
Five barley loaves	332
Foot washing song, The	121
For our life together we celebrate	305
For the fruit of the Spirit is love	179
For we are a chosen race	194
For you are my God	311
Freely, freely	227
Fruit of the Spirit, The	179
Gift of finest wheat	293
Give me oil in my lamp	4
Gloria, Gloria, Gloria	246
Glorious things of thee are spoken	69
Glory	150
Glory be to Jesus	65
Glory hallelujah!	245
Go forth and tell	92
Go tell everyone	89
Go tell it on the mountain	117
God and man at table are sat down	64
God forgave my sin in Jesus' name	227
God gives peace like a river	153
God has called [name]	70
God has called you	70
God has spoken	91
God himself is with us	22
God is building a house	58
God is for me	334
God is our Father	343
God is working his purpose out	88
God, make us your family	193
God of grace and God of glory	192
God's Spirit is in my heart	89
Good evening, Father	296
Good morning, Jesus	240
Good morning, this is the day	361
Great is thy faithfulness	312
Guide me, O thou great Jehovah	191
Hail, thou once despised Jesus	76
Hail to the Lord's anointed	129
Hallelujah, for the Lord our God	258
Hallelujah! Gonna sing all about it	132
Hallelujah! Hallelujah!	241
Hallelujah! Jesus is Lord!	15
Hallelujah, my father	133
Hallelujah . . . our God reigns	258
Hallelujah song	241
Hallelujah today	124
Hallowed be thy name	172
Harvest of righteousness	303
He is Lord	24
He is my everything	205
He shall teach you all things	40
He signed my deed	77
He will fill your hearts today	125
He who supplies seed to the sower	303
Here comes Jesus	47
Here he comes, robed in majesty	368
Here we are, Lord	300
He's able	307
He's my rock, my sword, my shield	222
Hey, [name], do you love Jesus?	105
Hiney mah tov	292
His name is wonderful	269
Ho! everyone that thirsteth	84
Holy Ghost Medley, The	73
Holy, holy	19
Hosanna, Lord!	366
Hosanna to the living King!	330
How beautiful the morning and the day	235
How firm a foundation	71

CELEBRATION

How great thou art	314
How lovely is thy dwelling place	358
How much greater	298
How sweet the name of Jesus sounds	46
Hymn of glory	245
Hymn to the Spirit	376
I am persuaded	202
I am so glad that Jesus loves me	207
I am so glad that our Father in heaven	207
I am the bread of life	60
I cannot come	111
I have decided to follow Jesus	74
I heard the Lord	80
I heard the voice of Jesus say	175
I know not why God's wondrous grace	315
I know whom I have believed	315
I lift up my soul	356
I looked up and I saw my Lord a-coming	270
I love the name of Jesus	148
I must have Jesus	217
I rejoiced when I heard them say	101
I sing a song of the saints of God	211
I sing to the shepherd of my soul	145
I trust in thee, O Lord	161
I walk with you	210
I want to live for Jesus every day	39
I want to walk as a child of the light	33
I want to walk with Jesus Christ	45
I will arise	159
I will arise and go to Jesus	274
I will dwell in his secret place	351
I will pour out my Spirit	367
I will praise the Lord with harp and string	330
I will rejoice	255
I will sing, I will sing	7
I will sing of the mercies	310
If I were a butterfly	102
If the eye say to the hand	107
If there's a mountain that needs to be moved	200
I'm not alone	218
In Christ there is no east or west	34
In the little town of Bethlehem	371
In the name of Jesus	197
In the presence of your people	254
Instrument song, The	339
Iona Gloria	246
Israel is my vineyard	182
Israel, rely on Yahweh	347
It makes no difference who you are	225
Jerusalem is fair	306
Jesu, Jesu, Fill us with your love	322
Jesus (SLW)	55
Jesus (CH)	261
Jesus came	272
Jesus Christ is alive today	16
Jesus gave her water	73
Jesus, I love you	143
Jesus is a-drivin' out Satan	199
Jesus is a friend of mine	110
Jesus is Lord!	78
Jesus is Lord, alleluia	267
Jesus is our King	289
Jesus is the one who saves	325
Jesus, Jesus	144
Jesus, Jesus is my Lord	103
Jesus, Jesus, Jesus	30
Jesus, Jesus loves [name]	209
Jesus, Jesus, wonderful Lord	31
Jesus, Lamb of God	167
Jesus loves Kristi	209
Jesus loves me	341
Jesus my Saviour	260
Jesus, name above all names	268
Jesus, never have I heard a name	30
Jesus shall reign	321
Jesus! the name high over all	232
Jesus, the very thought of thee	157
Jesus took my burdens	216
Jesus, your blood	259
Jesus, you're a wonder	265
Joy in the Lord	93
Jubilate Deo	352
Jubilate Deo	354
Jubilate Deo (round)	244
Jubilate, everybody	352
Knock, knock	212
Kum ba yah	41
Kyrie eleison	326
Let all that is within me	20
Let there be peace on earth	226
Let us break bread together	187
Let us give thanks	8
Let us praise the Lord with guitar	339
Let your light shine	118
Lift up your heads	357
Like the woman at the well	279
Litany	273
Living Lord	317
Lo! he comes	364
Look around you, can't you see?	326
Lord, give us your Spirit	286
Lord has done great things for us, The	95
Lord, I want to be a Christian	35
Lord Jesus Christ, You have come to us	317
Lord of all hopefulness	43
Lord, you have fulfilled your word	165
Lord's Prayer, The (FS)	171
Lord's Prayer, The (CH)	297
Love you, love you, Abba, Father	338
'Lu-ia, 'lu-ia	287
Make me a channel of your peace	223
Man of Galilee, The	177
Man of sorrows	363
Morning has broken	9
Morning Psalm	235
Moto Imeaka leo	229
My God	181
My God, how wonderful thou art	158
My hope is built	316
My Jesus, he saves and heals me	176
My Jesus, I love thee	155
My Lord, he is a-comin' soon	372
My sheep hear my voice	294
My song is love unknown	147
My soul doth magnify the Lord	166
Neighbours	322
Now let us sing	136
O, be joyful in the Lord	354
O Breath of Life	42
O clap your hands	239
O for a thousand tongues to sing (SLW)	17
O for a thousand tongues to sing (CH)	257
O give thanks unto the Lord	164
O Lord, all the world belongs to you	86
O Lord my God! When I in awesome wonder	314
O Lord, our God, We lift up our hearts to you	273
O Lord, our Lord, how great is your name in the earth	344
O Lord, your love is changing the world	328
O love, how deep	309
O magnify the Lord	162
O what a gift!	2
O welcome, all ye noble saints of old	64
O worship the Lord in the beauty of holiness	154
O Zion, haste	90
Oh! how good is the Lord	6
Oh, how I love Jesus	105
Oh, Mary, don't you weep	115
Oh, the blood of Jesus	61
On Christ the solid rock	316
On Jordan's bank	113
On Jordan's stormy banks	203
On Tiptoe	210
Once no people	194
One must water, one must weed	337
One, two, three, Jesus loves me	214
Our Father in heaven (FS)	171
Our Father in heaven (CH)	297
Our Father who art in heaven	172
Peace is flowing	87
Peace, perfect peace	275
Pentecost song, The	367
People of God	291
Peter and James and John	335
Peter and John went to pray	48
Planted wheat	127
Please break this bread, Lord	186
Praise God for the body	295
Praise God from whom all blessings flow	168, 169, 170
Praise him	14
Praise my God with the tambourine	134
Praise, my soul, the King of heaven	252
Praise the Lord	106
Praise to the Lord	11
Praise ye the Lord always	237
Prayer of St. Francis	223
Psalm 8	344
Psalm 84	358
Pullin' the weeds, Lord	213
Pure light	285

Title	No.
Put on love	174
Put on the apron of humility	121
Put on the whole armour of God	219
Put on your boots	215
Rain song	340
Reach out and touch the Lord	38
Rejoice in the Lord always	10
¡Resucitó, resucitó!	375
Robed in majesty	368
Sanna	128
Sea walker, The	85
See amid the winter's snow	116
See him a-lying on a bed of straw	114
See the conqueror mounts in triumph	75
Seed song, The	337
Seek ye first	56
Servant song, The	304
Shepherd of my soul, The	145
Silent night	331
Silver and Gold have I none	48
Sing a new song to the Lord	99
Sing a song, a joyful song	373
Sing hallelujah to the Father	318
Sing praise to the Lord for ever and ever	137
Sing, sing alleluia	138
Sing, sing, praise and sing!	106
Sing to our father	243
Sing to the Lord	139
Sing to the Lord	150
Sing unto the Lord	350
[Someone], Jesus loves you	208
Something in my heart	3
Son of God	21
Song of Simeon, The	165
Sorrow of Mary, The	362
Sound on the trumpet	278
Spirit divine	32
Spirit of the living God	29
Spirit, working in creation	376
Sweet Jesus (Anon.)	151
Sweet Jesus (Goodwin)	152
Take my hand and follow me	85
Tallis' Canon	169
Tell my people	284
Tell out, my soul	253
Thank you, Lord	109
Thank you, thank you, Jesus	18 & 27
The fear of the Lord	276
The fullness of the Godhead bodily	72
The God of Abraham praise	131
The joy of the Lord	79
The King of Glory comes	120
The King of love my shepherd is	68
The kingdom of God	59
The light of Christ	224
The Lord hath put a new song	96
The Lord is a great and mighty king	184
The Lord is my light	346
The Lord is my shepherd (SLW)	104
The Lord is my shepherd (CH)	348
The Lord is present	242
The Lord's my shepherd (SLW)	98
The Lord's my shepherd (CH)	345
The Spirit is a-movin'	228
The Spirit of the Lord	233
The steadfast love of the Lord	173
There is a balm in Gilead	49
There is a river	163
There is power in the blood	176
There's a new song in the land	288
There's a quiet understanding	271
There's a river of praise	249
There's a wideness in God's mercy	323
There's new life in Jesus	333
They cast their nets in Galilee	206
They say that I'm a dreamer	177
They that wait upon the Lord	280
Thine be the glory	123
This is my commandment	67
This is the day	13
This is the day of the Lord	141
This is the feast	185
This, this is the day	248
Those who trust in the Lord	349
Thou art worthy	28
Thou wilt keep him in perfect peace	183
Thy lovingkindness	353
To you, Yahweh, I lift up my soul	356
Triumphant Zion	189
Trust in the Lord	277
Turn me, O God	142
Turn your eyes upon Jesus	156
Wake up!	112
We are coming, Lord	299
We cry, 'Hosanna, Lord'	366
We love the Lord	108
We must follow the Lord	336
We really want to thank you, Lord	66
We see the Lord	23
We want to bless you	236
We will sing to the Lord our God	140
Wedding banquet, The	111
Well, come go with me to that land	204
Were you there	122
What could be better	190
What wondrous love is this	119
When I survey the wondrous cross (FS)	201
When I survey the wondrous cross (CH)	262
When Jesus met with his disciples	230
When led by the Spirit	319
When the Lord came	329
When the Lord restored	95
Wherever two or more	196
Who are my mother and my brothers?	188
Who does Jesus love	320
Whosoever will	308
Wind, wind	178
Wondrous love	119
Won't you come?	327
Worthy the Lamb	263
You are my witnesses	324
You gotta have love in your heart	51
You satisfy the hungry heart	293
Your kingdom come, your will be done	193
Your love is changing the world	328